The Sonnets of William Shakespeare
In Plain and Simple English

William Shakespeare

SwipeSpeare™
www.SwipeSpeare.com

Table of Contents

About This Series

The "Classic Retold" series started as a way of telling classics for the modern reader—being careful to preserve the themes and integrity of the original. Whether you want to understand Shakespeare a little more or are trying to get a better grasps of the Greek classics, there is a book waiting for you!

The series is expanding every month. Visit BookCaps.com to see all the books in the series, and while you are there join the Facebook page, so you are first to know when a new book comes out.

Sonnets

Sonnet I

From fairest creatures we desire increase,
That thereby beauty's rose might never die,
But as the riper should by time decease,
His tender heir might bear his memory:
But thou, contracted to thine own bright eyes,
Feed'st thy light'st flame with self-substantial fuel,
Making a famine where abundance lies,
Thyself thy foe, to thy sweet self too cruel.
Thou that art now the world's fresh ornament
And only herald to the gaudy spring,
Within thine own bud buriest thy content
And, tender churl, makest waste in niggarding.
Pity the world, or else this glutton be,
To eat the world's due, by the grave and thee.

We want beautiful people to reproduce,
So their beauty will never die,
And as the parent grows older and his looks decrease,
His beautiful child will bear the memory of his youth,
But you, caught up with your own sparkling eyes,
Feed upon your own beauty and burn it out,
Making very little where a lot should be.
You are your own worst enemy and cruel in your sweetness.
You are, for the time being, a good looking young person,
and a messenger of the brilliance of spring itself,
But you keep your loveliness to yourself,
And—young and ungracious—you waste it by hoarding it.
Take pity on the world or you will be seen as greedy,
Having taken all of your beauty to the grave with you.

Sonnet II

When forty winters shall beseige thy brow,
And dig deep trenches in thy beauty's field,
Thy youth's proud livery, so gazed on now,
Will be a tatter'd weed, of small worth held:
Then being ask'd where all thy beauty lies,
Where all the treasure of thy lusty days,
To say, within thine own deep-sunken eyes,
Were an all-eating shame and thriftless praise.
How much more praise deserved thy beauty's
use,
If thou couldst answer 'This fair child of mine
Shall sum my count and make my old excuse,'
Proving his beauty by succession thine!
This were to be new made when thou art old,
And see thy blood warm when thou feel'st it
cold.

When forty years have overtaken your brow,
And have dug deep wrinkles in its smooth
beauty,
The proud costume of your youth viewed now,
Will be a tattered weed that is worthless.
And when you are asked where is your beauty—
What happened to the prize of your younger
days?
If you were to say it's within your deep sunken
eyes,
It would be a shameful and useless praise.
How much better if your beauty had been spent
having a child,
So that you could answer 'This child of mine
Accounts for why I look so old.'
Your beauty would be passed on through him!
This would make you appear new when you are
old,
And his blood would still be warm when yours
cools.

Sonnet III

Look in thy glass, and tell the face thou viewest
Now is the time that face should form another;
Whose fresh repair if now thou not renewest,
Thou dost beguile the world, unbless some mother.
For where is she so fair whose unear'd womb
Disdains the tillage of thy husbandry?
Or who is he so fond will be the tomb
Of his self-love, to stop posterity?
Thou art thy mother's glass, and she in thee
Calls back the lovely April of her prime:
So thou through windows of thine age shall see
Despite of wrinkles this thy golden time.
But if thou live, remember'd not to be,
Die single, and thine image dies with thee.

*Look in your mirror and tell the face looking
back at you
That now is the time to bear a child with the
same face.
Your face is fresh and young now, but if you
don't regenerate it
You will cheat the world and deprive a mother.
Who out there is so beautiful that her womb
Would refuse to take the seed of your child?
And who is so foolish that he will be the death,
Due to his self-obsession, of his own line of
descendants?
Your own face is your mother's mirror, and she
sees in it
The lovely springtime of her youth.
You will also be able to look back in your old
age
And see your youth in your child's face despite
your wrinkles.
But if you live without having children, you will
not be remembered.
You will die alone, and your image will die with
you.*

Sonnet IV

Unthrifty loveliness, why dost thou spend
Upon thyself thy beauty's legacy?
Nature's bequest gives nothing but doth lend,
And being frank she lends to those are free.
Then, beauteous niggard, why dost thou abuse
The bounteous largess given thee to give?
Profitless usurer, why dost thou use
So great a sum of sums, yet canst not live?
For having traffic with thyself alone,
Thou of thyself thy sweet self dost deceive.
Then how, when nature calls thee to be gone,
What acceptable audit canst thou leave?
Thy unused beauty must be tomb'd with thee,
Which, used, lives th' executor to be.

Wasteful beautiful person, why do you spend
All of your beauty on yourself?
Nature gives nothing but she lends a lot,
And, being generous, she lends most to those
who are carefree.
So, you miserly hoarder, why do you abuse
The open-hearted gift given to you?
You make no profit, so why do you use
So much of your gift when you can't live on
forever?
Your dealings are with yourself alone,
And only you alone receive the sweet gift of
yourself.
When nature calls you to die,
What account of your life will you leave behind?
Your unused beauty will go to the grave with
you,
And, if it had been used, it could carry on.

Sonnet V

Those hours, that with gentle work did frame
The lovely gaze where every eye doth dwell,
Will play the tyrants to the very same
And that unfair which fairly doth excel:
For never-resting time leads summer on
To hideous winter and confounds him there;
Sap cheque'd with frost and lusty leaves quite gone,
Beauty o'ersnow'd and bareness every where:
Then, were not summer's distillation left,
A liquid prisoner pent in walls of glass,
Beauty's effect with beauty were bereft,
Nor it nor no remembrance what it was:
But flowers distill'd though they with winter meet,
Leese but their show; their substance still lives sweet.

The same process of time that gently works to create
The beauty of the face that holds everyone's gaze,
Will do cruel work to the same face
And make it ugly even though it is now so beautiful.
Time never rests and it leads summer on
Into frightful winter and destroys it there,
Freezing its sap and taking away its vigourous leaves,
Covering it over with snow and bareness everywhere.
If summer's essence had not been left behind
As a liquid perfume contained in glass,
There would be nothing left of its beauty,
And no memory of what it had been.
But flowers made into perfume before winter arrives,
Lose only their appearance: their sweet scent remains.

Sonnet VI

Then let not winter's ragged hand deface
In thee thy summer, ere thou be distill'd:
Make sweet some vial; treasure thou some place
With beauty's treasure, ere it be self-kill'd.
That use is not forbidden usury,
Which happies those that pay the willing loan;
That's for thyself to breed another thee,
Or ten times happier, be it ten for one;
Ten times thyself were happier than thou art,
If ten of thine ten times refigured thee:
Then what could death do, if thou shouldst depart,
Leaving thee living in posterity?
Be not self-will'd, for thou art much too fair
To be death's conquest and make worms thine heir.

Don't allow winter's rough hand to disfigure
The summer beauty in you before it is distilled—
Make it into something sweet that can be contained
Like a treasure before you ruin it.
It is not a forbidden use of interest—
A willing woman would be happy to repay the loan
And produce a child for you,
Or ten times happier, if there were ten children.
You yourself would be ten times happier
If you had ten children who looked like you.
What can death do to you then, if you should die
Leaving yourself living on in your descendants?
Don't be selfish—you are too beautiful
To allow death to conquer you and leave you to the worms.

Sonnet VII

Lo! in the orient when the gracious light
Lifts up his burning head, each under eye
Doth homage to his new-appearing sight,
Serving with looks his sacred majesty;
And having climb'd the steep-up heavenly hill,
Resembling strong youth in his middle age,
yet mortal looks adore his beauty still,
Attending on his golden pilgrimage;
But when from highmost pitch, with weary car,
Like feeble age, he reeleth from the day,
The eyes, 'fore duteous, now converted are
From his low tract and look another way:
So thou, thyself out-going in thy noon,
Unlook'd on diest, unless thou get a son.

Look! When the gracious light of the sun
rises in the east, everyone looks
And acknowledges its newness with respect,
Watching it like a king.
Once it has climbed the high and heavenly hill
of noon,
It still looks like a strong young man in his
prime
And people still admire its beauty,
And pay attention to its golden passage.
But when the weary chariot begins to fall from
the highest point,
And becomes unsteady and reels like an old
man,
Then the eyes, which were dutiful before, look
away
From it at this low point into another direction.
You too, who is beginning to leave your youth
behind,
Will not be looked at when you die, unless you
father a son.

Sonnet VIII

Music to hear, why hear'st thou music sadly?
Sweets with sweets war not, joy delights in joy.
Why lovest thou that which thou receivest not
gladly,
Or else receivest with pleasure thine annoy?
If the true concord of well-tuned sounds,
By unions married, do offend thine ear,
They do but sweetly chide thee, who confounds
In singleness the parts that thou shouldst bear.
Mark how one string, sweet husband to another,
Strikes each in each by mutual ordering,
Resembling sire and child and happy mother
Who all in one, one pleasing note do sing:
Whose speechless song, being many, seeming
one,
Sings this to thee: 'thou single wilt prove none.'

*Why does listening to music make you feel so
sad?*
*Sweetness usually finds peace with sweetness,
and joy delights in joy.*
*Why do you love that which makes you unhappy,
And enjoy the things that bring you trouble?*
*If the harmony of music that's in tune
And played well offends you,
It is because it scolds you for challenging it
By not taking the part you should take.
Listen to how one string, when sweetly married
to another,
Strikes in well-matched order and harmony,
Like a father and child and happy mother,
Who sing one pleasing note together.
Their wordless song, being many but seeming as
one,
Sings to you: 'you'll have nothing if you stay
alone.'*

Sonnet IX

Is it for fear to wet a widow's eye
That thou consumest thyself in single life?
Ah! if thou issueless shalt hap to die.
The world will wail thee, like a makeless wife;
The world will be thy widow and still weep
That thou no form of thee hast left behind,
When every private widow well may keep
By children's eyes her husband's shape in mind.
Look, what an unthrift in the world doth spend
Shifts but his place, for still the world enjoys it;
But beauty's waste hath in the world an end,
And kept unused, the user so destroys it.
No love toward others in that bosom sits
That on himself such murderous shame
commits.

Is it because you fear to make a widow cry
That you continue to live the single life?
Oh! But if you happen to die childless,
The world will cry for you like a husbandless
wife;
The world will be your widow and will cry,
Because you will not have left a likeness of
yourself behind,
As is the case with every other widow who can
see
Her husband's image in her children's eyes.
Look, when a spendthrift wastes money
It just changes hands, but it is still here for the
world to enjoy.
But if beauty is wasted, it leaves the world—
By not using it, the user destroys it.
There is no love for others in the heart
Of someone who commits such a murderous
disgrace.

Sonnet X

For shame! deny that thou bear'st love to any,	It's a disgrace that you refuse to admit love for anyone
Who for thyself art so unprovident.	It's thoughtless and won't provide for the future.
Grant, if thou wilt, thou art beloved of many,	It's true, admit it, that many people love you,
But that thou none lovest is most evident;	And that you love no one is obvious.
For thou art so possess'd with murderous hate	You are so full of murderous hate
That 'gainst thyself thou stick'st not to conspire.	That you don't even hesitate to plot against yourself.
Seeking that beauteous roof to ruinate	You seek to destroy the beautiful roof over your head
Which to repair should be thy chief desire.	When its repair is what you should be seeking.
O, change thy thought, that I may change my mind!	Oh, change your way of thinking so that I may change my mind!
Shall hate be fairer lodged than gentle love?	Should hate be cared for better than gentle love?
Be, as thy presence is, gracious and kind,	Be like you appear to be—gracious and kind,
Or to thyself at least kind-hearted prove:	Or at least be kind-hearted to yourself:
Make thee another self, for love of me,	Have a child, out of love for me,
That beauty still may live in thine or thee.	So that your beauty may still live on in your children.

Sonnet XI

As fast as thou shalt wane, so fast thou growest
In one of thine, from that which thou departest;
And that fresh blood which youngly thou bestowest
Thou mayst call thine when thou from youth convertest.
Herein lives wisdom, beauty and increase:
Without this, folly, age and cold decay:
If all were minded so, the times should cease
And threescore year would make the world away.
Let those whom Nature hath not made for store,
Harsh featureless and rude, barrenly perish:
Look, whom she best endow'd she gave the more;
Which bounteous gift thou shouldst in bounty cherish:
She carved thee for her seal, and meant thereby
Thou shouldst print more, not let that copy die.

As quickly as you decline, you could grow just as quickly
In one of your children, although you depart.
The fresh blood you passed on in your youth
You could call your own when you are no longer young.
Having children brings wisdom, beauty and descendants.
Not having children only brings lewdness, old age and decay.
If everyone thought as you do, society would stop,
And in sixty years, the world would end.
Let those who Nature made unfit for reproduction—
The rough, ugly and offensive—go childless.
Look, the ones Nature gave the most to have more,
And the generous gift should be well looked after.
She carved her seal in you and meant for you
To reproduce and make copies so the original does not die.

Sonnet XII

When I do count the clock that tells the time,
And see the brave day sunk in hideous night;
When I behold the violet past prime,
And sable curls all silver'd o'er with white;
When lofty trees I see barren of leaves
Which erst from heat did canopy the herd,
And summer's green all girded up in sheaves
Borne on the bier with white and bristly beard,
Then of thy beauty do I question make,
That thou among the wastes of time must go,
Since sweets and beauties do themselves forsake
And die as fast as they see others grow;
And nothing 'gainst Time's scythe can make defence
Save breed, to brave him when he takes thee hence.

When I look at the clock and see time passing,
And watch as the splendid day sinks into terrifying night,
When I see the violets fade,
And black curls turn to gray,
When tall trees become bare
That once provided shade during heat for the herds,
And summer's crops are tied up in sheaves,
And carried away like a white bearded old man in a coffin,
Then I wonder about your beauty,
That you are allowing to go to waste with time.
Sweet and beautiful things all decline
And die as quickly as they watch others grow.
There's nothing you can do to avoid Time cutting you down,
Except to bear children to carry on after you die.

Sonnet XIII

O, that you were yourself! but, love, you are
No longer yours than you yourself here live:
Against this coming end you should prepare,
And your sweet semblance to some other give.
So should that beauty which you hold in lease
Find no determination: then you were
Yourself again after yourself's decease,
When your sweet issue your sweet form should
bear.
Who lets so fair a house fall to decay,
Which husbandry in honour might uphold
Against the stormy gusts of winter's day
And barren rage of death's eternal cold?
O, none but unthrifts! Dear my love, you know
You had a father: let your son say so.

Oh, if only you were yourself! But, my love, you are
only yourself for as long as you live.
You should prepare for the inevitable end
By having a child to carry on your sweet appearance
So that the beauty you have for the time being
Does not end. Then you would be
Yourself again, after you yourself decrease,
Since your child would have your good looks.
Who lets a beautiful house fall to ruin,
That careful management might maintain
Against the stormy winds of a winter day,
And the empty violence of death's eternal cold?
Nobody but a spendthrift! My dear, you know
You had a father. Let your son be able to say the same.

Sonnet XIV

Not from the stars do I my judgment pluck;
And yet methinks I have astronomy,
But not to tell of good or evil luck,
Of plagues, of dearths, or seasons' quality;
Nor can I fortune to brief minutes tell,
Pointing to each his thunder, rain and wind,
Or say with princes if it shall go well,
By oft predict that I in heaven find:
But from thine eyes my knowledge I derive,
And, constant stars, in them I read such art
As truth and beauty shall together thrive,
If from thyself to store thou wouldst convert;
Or else of thee this I prognosticate:
Thy end is truth's and beauty's doom and date.

I don't draw knowledge from the stars,
And yet I think I do know a little about
astrology.
Not enough to predict good or bad luck,
Or to be able to foresee plagues, famines, or the
way a season will be,
And I can't see to the minute what will happen—
Predicting every thunder, rain and wind,
Nor am I able to tell princes how things will go
By looking at the heavens.
I gain my knowledge from looking in your eyes,
And—like steady stars—I can read in them
That beauty and truth will thrive together
If you should decide to have children.
Otherwise, all I can foretell for you is:
Your truth and beauty will die with you.

Sonnet XV

When I consider every thing that grows
Holds in perfection but a little moment,
That this huge stage presenteth nought but shows
Whereon the stars in secret influence comment;
When I perceive that men as plants increase,
Cheered and cheque'd even by the self-same sky,
Vaunt in their youthful sap, at height decrease,
And wear their brave state out of memory;
Then the conceit of this inconstant stay
Sets you most rich in youth before my sight,
Where wasteful Time debateth with Decay,
To change your day of youth to sullied night;
And all in war with Time for love of you,
As he takes from you, I engraft you new.

When I consider how everything that grows,
Is only perfect for a brief time,
And that this world is like a huge stage
presenting nothing but shows
That are secretly influenced by the stars,
When I think about how men grow just like
plants—
Encouraged and restrained under the same sky
Proud in their vital youth but decreasing as they
reach their highest point,
Keeping nothing of their excellence that
eventually is forgotten.
Then the thought of this inconstant state of
things
Makes you seem so rich with youth in my eyes.
I see wasteful Time debating with Death
About how to change your youth into old age;
Out of love, I am in war with Time for you,
And as he takes from you, I try to divide you
anew.

Sonnet XVI

But wherefore do not you a mightier way
Make war upon this bloody tyrant, Time?
And fortify yourself in your decay
With means more blessed than my barren rhyme?
Now stand you on the top of happy hours,
And many maiden gardens yet unset
With virtuous wish would bear your living flowers,
Much liker than your painted counterfeit:
So should the lines of life that life repair,
Which this, Time's pencil, or my pupil pen,
Neither in inward worth nor outward fair,
Can make you live yourself in eyes of men.
To give away yourself keeps yourself still,
And you must live, drawn by your own sweet skill.

But why don't you find a mightier way
To make war upon this bloody tyrant, Time?
And strengthen yourself as you age
With ways happier than my stupid poems?
You are at the height of your happy youth,
And many fertile and young women
Of virtue would love to marry you and bear your children
That would look more like you than a painting.
And the lines of your life would be restored,
Which neither Time itself nor my apprentice pen
In inner worth or outward beauty,
Can do like you can do yourself by having children.
Giving yourself away allows you to keep yourself,
And you will live on, carried by your own pleasing common sense.

Sonnet XVII

Who will believe my verse in time to come,
If it were fill'd with your most high deserts?
Though yet, heaven knows, it is but as a tomb
Which hides your life and shows not half your parts.
If I could write the beauty of your eyes
And in fresh numbers number all your graces,
The age to come would say 'This poet lies:
Such heavenly touches ne'er touch'd earthly faces.'
So should my papers yellow'd with their age
Be scorn'd like old men of less truth than tongue,
And your true rights be term'd a poet's rage
And stretched metre of an antique song:
But were some child of yours alive that time,
You should live twice; in it and in my rhyme.

Who will believe my poems in years to come,
If I write about your highest merits?
As it is, heaven knows, my poems are like a tomb
That hide your life and do not show the half of you.
If I could capture how beautiful your eyes are in words,
And manage to list all of your good qualities,
The time would come when people say 'This poet lies:
There's no way such heavenly things were seen in human faces.'
And so my poems, their pages yellowed with age,
Would be scorned like old men who talk a lot but don't speak true,
And your rightful claim would be called a poet's madness,
The false lines of an old song.
But if you had a child still alive at that time,
You would live twice: in your child and in my rhymes.

Sonnet XVIII

Shall I compare thee to a summer's day?
Thou art more lovely and more temperate:
Rough winds do shake the darling buds of May,
And summer's lease hath all too short a date:
Sometime too hot the eye of heaven shines,
And often is his gold complexion dimm'd;
And every fair from fair sometime declines,
By chance or nature's changing course untrimm'd;
But thy eternal summer shall not fade
Nor lose possession of that fair thou owest;
Nor shall Death brag thou wander'st in his shade,
When in eternal lines to time thou growest:
So long as men can breathe or eyes can see,
So long lives this and this gives life to thee.

Should I compare you to a summer day?
You are lovelier and calmer:
Rough winds shake the precious buds of May,
And summer does not last very long.
Sometimes the sun overhead is too hot,
And often its golden light is dimmed,
And every thing that is beautiful loses its beauty,
Either by accident or simply because of the due course of Nature.
But your eternal summer will not fade,
And you will not lose possession of your beauty.
Death will not brag that you are wandering in his underworld,
When in these eternal lines you exist.
As long as men can breathe or eyes can see,
As long as this poem exists, you will live.

Sonnet XIX

Devouring Time, blunt thou the lion's paws,
And make the earth devour her own sweet brood;
Pluck the keen teeth from the fierce tiger's jaws,
And burn the long-lived phoenix in her blood;
Make glad and sorry seasons as thou fleets,
And do whate'er thou wilt, swift-footed Time,
To the wide world and all her fading sweets;
But I forbid thee one most heinous crime:
O, carve not with thy hours my love's fair brow,
Nor draw no lines there with thine antique pen;
Him in thy course untainted do allow
For beauty's pattern to succeeding men.
Yet, do thy worst, old Time: despite thy wrong,
My love shall in my verse ever live young.

Devouring Time, you can blunt the lion's paws,
And make the earth readily consume her children.
You can create joyful and sorrowful times as you pass,
And do whatever you will, swift-footed Time,
To the whole world and all its fading delights,
But I forbid you to commit the one most terrible crime:
Do not carve your hours into my love's beautiful forehead,
Or draw any lines there with your antique pen.
Let him to go unmarked by you and allow
Him to serve as a pattern of beauty for men to come.
Still, do your worst, old Time, and despite your doing so
My love will be forever young in my poetry.

Sonnet XX

A woman's face with Nature's own hand painted
Hast thou, the master-mistress of my passion;
A woman's gentle heart, but not acquainted
With shifting change, as is false women's
fashion;
An eye more bright than theirs, less false in
rolling,
Gilding the object whereupon it gazeth;
A man in hue, all 'hues' in his controlling,
Much steals men's eyes and women's souls
amazeth.
And for a woman wert thou first created;
Till Nature, as she wrought thee, fell a-doting,
And by addition me of thee defeated,
By adding one thing to my purpose nothing.
But since she prick'd thee out for women's
pleasure,
Mine be thy love and thy love's use their
treasure.

Nature has painted a woman's face with her
own hand
On you, the master and mistress of my passion.
And she gave you a woman's gentle heart, but it
does not
Change quickly, as a disloyal woman's tends to
do.
Your eyes are brighter than a woman's, with no
unfaithful expression,
And everything you look at becomes more
beautiful.
Your appearance as a man who has mastered
his looks,
Stealthily captures the glances of men and
amazes the souls of women.
You were first created as a woman
Until Nature, seeing what she created, fell for
you
And she added something to defeat my having
you
By giving you one thing I have no use for.
So since she gave you a prick in order to please
women,
I will have your love and they can love your
treasure.

Sonnet XXI

So is it not with me as with that Muse
Stirr'd by a painted beauty to his verse,
Who heaven itself for ornament doth use
And every fair with his fair doth rehearse
Making a couplement of proud compare,
With sun and moon, with earth and sea's rich gems,
With April's first-born flowers, and all things rare
That heaven's air in this huge rondure hems.
O' let me, true in love, but truly write,
And then believe me, my love is as fair
As any mother's child, though not so bright
As those gold candles fix'd in heaven's air:
Let them say more than like of hearsay well;
I will not praise that purpose not to sell.

It is not like me to be like the poet who,
Inspired to write poetry by a woman wearing make-up,
Says she has the quality of heaven
And then compares her with every beautiful thing by
Joining her with them in splendid similes.
She is like the sun, the moon, and all the treasures of earth and sea,
Like April's first flowers and all things rare
That are contained within heaven and on earth.
Let me, since I'm truly in love, write faithfully,
And then you can believe—my love is as beautiful
As any child is to its mother, although not as bright
As the golden stars fixed in the sky.
Let those who like that sort of thing say more.
It is not my intention to sell, so I won't overpraise.

Sonnet XXII

My glass shall not persuade me I am old,
So long as youth and thou are of one date;
But when in thee time's furrows I behold,
Then look I death my days should expiate.
For all that beauty that doth cover thee
Is but the seemly raiment of my heart,
Which in thy breast doth live, as thine in me:
How can I then be elder than thou art?
O, therefore, love, be of thyself so wary
As I, not for myself, but for thee will;
Bearing thy heart, which I will keep so chary
As tender nurse her babe from faring ill.
Presume not on thy heart when mine is slain;
Thou gavest me thine, not to give back again.

My mirror will not convince me I am old,
As long as you look youthful.
But when I see time's furrows unfold in you,
Then I know my death is approaching.
All of the beauty that covers you
Is the clothing I wear close to my heart:
It lives inside me, as you live inside me.
How could I ever be older than you?
Oh, therefore, my love, watch over yourself
As carefully as I do, which I do
Because I have your heart. I keep it as dearly
As a nurse keeps her baby from harm.
Don't expect to get your heart back when mine
is destroyed.
You gave it to me, and I can't give it back.

Sonnet XXIII

As an unperfect actor on the stage
Who with his fear is put besides his part,
Or some fierce thing replete with too much rage,
Whose strength's abundance weakens his own heart.
So I, for fear of trust, forget to say
The perfect ceremony of love's rite,
And in mine own love's strength seem to decay,
O'ercharged with burden of mine own love's might.
O, let my books be then the eloquence
And dumb presagers of my speaking breast,
Who plead for love and look for recompense
More than that tongue that more hath more express'd.
O, learn to read what silent love hath writ:
To hear with eyes belongs to love's fine wit.

Like an unskilled actor on the stage,
Who can't remember his part due to fear,
Or like some wild thing filled with too much rage,
Whose abundance of strength weakens his heart,
So I, out of fear of trusting myself, forget to express
The perfect words to symbolize love's ceremony.
And so it seems the strength of my love makes me decline,
And I am overburdened with the weight of it.
So let the words in my books be eloquent—
Let them be silent interpreters of what is in my heart,
And they can plead for love and look for reward,
More than what my tongue can express.
Learn to read what silent love has written,
And to hear with your eyes love's exquisitely formed thoughts.

Sonnet XXIV

Mine eye hath play'd the painter and hath stell'd
Thy beauty's form in table of my heart;
My body is the frame wherein 'tis held,
And perspective it is the painter's art.
For through the painter must you see his skill,
To find where your true image pictured lies;
Which in my bosom's shop is hanging still,
That hath his windows glazed with thine eyes.
Now see what good turns eyes for eyes have done:
Mine eyes have drawn thy shape, and thine for me
Are windows to my breast, where-through the sun
Delights to peep, to gaze therein on thee;
Yet eyes this cunning want to grace their art;
They draw but what they see, know not the heart.

My eyes have been like a painter and have portrayed
The shape of your beauty in the notebook of my heart.
My body is the frame that holds your image,
And I keep it in perspective like an artist.
The painter's skill will help you to see,
Where your true image resides,
Which hangs in my heart's workshop,
As your eyes stare into me.
Look what good our eyes have done for each other:
My eyes have drawn your shape, and your eyes
Have looked into my heart, where the sun
Also likes to look, and gaze upon you.
Still, my cunning eyes lack grace in their art:
They draw what they see, but they do not know your heart.

Sonnet XXV

Let those who are in favour with their stars
Of public honour and proud titles boast,
Whilst I, whom fortune of such triumph bars,
Unlook'd for joy in that I honour most.
Great princes' favourites their fair leaves spread
But as the marigold at the sun's eye,
And in themselves their pride lies buried,
For at a frown they in their glory die.
The painful warrior famoused for fight,
After a thousand victories once foil'd,
Is from the book of honour razed quite,
And all the rest forgot for which he toil'd:
Then happy I, that love and am beloved
Where I may not remove nor be removed.

Let those who are lucky
Have public honor and titles they can brag
about,
While I, who am not fortunate enough to have
the glory,
Have found joy in an honor I did not expect.
The favorites of great princes spread their
leaves,
And flower like a marigold in the hot sun—
Their pride lies buried within them,
But their glory will die at a simple frown.
The warrior who has endured pain and is
famous for his fights,
Defeated only once after a thousand victories,
Is completely cut from the book of honor,
And all of the battles he won are forgotten.
I am happy, then, to love and be loved,
And to be in a place I will not leave or be
removed from.

Sonnet XXVI

Lord of my love, to whom in vassalage
Thy merit hath my duty strongly knit,
To thee I send this written embassage,
To witness duty, not to show my wit:
Duty so great, which wit so poor as mine
May make seem bare, in wanting words to show
it,
But that I hope some good conceit of thine
In thy soul's thought, all naked, will bestow it;
Till whatsoever star that guides my moving
Points on me graciously with fair aspect
And puts apparel on my tatter'd loving,
To show me worthy of thy sweet respect:
Then may I dare to boast how I do love thee;
Till then not show my head where thou mayst
prove me.

My noble love, I am in service to you—
Your worth has tied me to you in duty.
I'm sending you this message
To show my duty to you, not my intelligence,
A duty that is great, although my lack of
intelligence
May make it seem simple without the right
words to show it.
But I hope you will be able to get a good idea,
Somewhere in your soul, of what I mean.
When the star that guides my movement,
Shines on me with divine grace and favorable
influence,
And dresses up my ragged way of loving,
And shows me worthy of your sweet respect:
Then will I be able to boast how much I love
you.
Until then, I will not show my face where you
might test me.

Sonnet XXVII

Weary with toil, I haste me to my bed,
The dear repose for limbs with travel tired;
But then begins a journey in my head,
To work my mind, when body's work's expired:
For then my thoughts, from far where I abide,
Intend a zealous pilgrimage to thee,
And keep my drooping eyelids open wide,
Looking on darkness which the blind do see
Save that my soul's imaginary sight
Presents thy shadow to my sightless view,
Which, like a jewel hung in ghastly night,
Makes black night beauteous and her old face new.
Lo! thus, by day my limbs, by night my mind,
For thee and for myself no quiet find.

Weary from work, I hurry to my bed—
The precious place of rest for legs tired with travel.
But then a journey begins in my head,
That stirs my mind when my body's work is done:
And then my thoughts go far from where I am,
And take a direct and enthusiastic journey to you.
I keep my drooping eyelids wide open,
Staring into the darkness like a blind person.
Except the heart of my imagination
Shows your image to my sightless view,
And it hangs like a jewel in the terrible night,
Making black night beautiful and her old face fresh.
So it is, by day my legs and by night my mind
Seek you and find no peace.

Sonnet XXVIII

How can I then return in happy plight,
That am debarr'd the benefit of rest?
When day's oppression is not eased by night,
But day by night, and night by day, oppress'd?
And each, though enemies to either's reign,
Do in consent shake hands to torture me;
The one by toil, the other to complain
How far I toil, still farther off from thee.
I tell the day, to please them thou art bright
And dost him grace when clouds do blot the
heaven:
So flatter I the swart-complexion'd night,
When sparkling stars twire not thou gild'st the
even.
But day doth daily draw my sorrows longer
And night doth nightly make grief's strength
seem stronger.

How can I return happy and in good shape
When I am deprived from getting any rest?
When the burdens of the day are not eased at
night,
But, instead, day burdens night and night
burdens day?
And each of them, although enemies to each
other,
Decide to agree to torture me together—
The one by tiring me out and the other spent
complaining
About how tired I am, and still so far away from
you.
I tell the day to please it that you are bright
And make the day good when clouds cover the
sun:
And I flatter the dark complexioned night by
saying
That when the sparkling stars do not twinkle you
still brighten the evening.
But day does daily make my sadness longer
And night does nightly make my grief seem
stronger.

Sonnet XXIX

When, in disgrace with fortune and men's eyes,
I all alone beweep my outcast state
And trouble deaf heaven with my bootless cries
And look upon myself and curse my fate,
Wishing me like to one more rich in hope,
Featured like him, like him with friends possess'd,
Desiring this man's art and that man's scope,
With what I most enjoy contented least;
Yet in these thoughts myself almost despising,
Haply I think on thee, and then my state,
Like to the lark at break of day arising
From sullen earth, sings hymns at heaven's gate;
For thy sweet love remember'd such wealth brings
That then I scorn to change my state with kings.

When I feel unfortunate and am seen as a disgrace by others,
I cry by myself about being an outcast
And disturb the deaf heavens with my useless cries,
And look at myself and curse my luck,
Wishing myself to be more like one who is hopeful,
And wishing I looked like him and had his friends.
I wish I had this man's skill and that man's opportunities,
And am unhappy with what usually makes me glad.
Still, when I have these thoughts and despise myself,
I happen to think of you and then my sense of well-being
Rises like a lark at the break of day
From the gloomy earth, singing hymns at heaven's gate.
The thought of your sweet love brings such wealth
That I would refuse to change places with kings.

Sonnet XXX

When to the sessions of sweet silent thought
I summon up remembrance of things past,
I sigh the lack of many a thing I sought,
And with old woes new wail my dear time's waste:
Then can I drown an eye, unused to flow,
For precious friends hid in death's dateless night,
And weep afresh love's long since cancell'd woe,
And moan the expense of many a vanish'd sight:
Then can I grieve at grievances foregone,
And heavily from woe to woe tell o'er
The sad account of fore-bemoaned moan,
Which I new pay as if not paid before.
But if the while I think on thee, dear friend,
All losses are restored and sorrows end.

When I'm alone with my sweet silent thoughts,
And I call up the memory of things from the past,
I sigh about not having gotten the things I tried to find,
And I cry about all the time I've wasted.
Then I can drown my eyes that are unused to tears
For friends who have passed into death's eternal night,
And weep again about loves I was sad about losing before,
And cry about how much the things that are gone have cost me.
I can sob heavily while I go over every sadness I've ever had,
Taking account of my previous sadnesess all over again,
And I cry about them as if I had not cried before.
But if I think about you while doing this, dear friend,
Then my losses are returned and my sadness ends.

Sonnet XXXI

Thy bosom is endeared with all hearts,
Which I by lacking have supposed dead,
And there reigns love and all love's loving parts,
And all those friends which I thought buried.
How many a holy and obsequious tear
Hath dear religious love stol'n from mine eye
As interest of the dead, which now appear
But things removed that hidden in thee lie!
Thou art the grave where buried love doth live,
Hung with the trophies of my lovers gone,
Who all their parts of me to thee did give;
That due of many now is thine alone:
Their images I loved I view in thee,
And thou, all they, hast all the all of me.

You have the hearts of everyone in your heart
Who I viewed as good as dead since I no longer
have them.
And there you have power over love and all its
qualities,
And all those friends I thought I had buried.
Many virtuous and dutiful tears
Have been stolen from my eye by dear, religious
love
And cried for the dead, who now appear
As things that were removed and hidden in you!
You are the grave where buried love lies,
And in it hangs the trophies of all my departed
lovers,
Who gave all of themselves to you.
What was due to me is now yours alone.
I can see everyone I've loved in you,
And you, who have everyone I've ever loved,
also has all of me.

Sonnet XXXII

If thou survive my well-contented day,
When that churl Death my bones with dust shall
cover,
And shalt by fortune once more re-survey
These poor rude lines of thy deceased lover,
Compare them with the bettering of the time,
And though they be outstripp'd by every pen,
Reserve them for my love, not for their rhyme,
Exceeded by the height of happier men.
O, then vouchsafe me but this loving thought:
'Had my friend's Muse grown with this growing
age,
A dearer birth than this his love had brought,
To march in ranks of better equipage:
But since he died and poets better prove,
Theirs for their style I'll read, his for his love.'

If you live on after I am gone
After Death has covered my bones with dust,
And you should happen to re-read
These poor, rough lines written by your dead
lover,
You will compare them with the better poems of
the time.
Although the poems written by the pens of those
poets will be better,
Look at mine for the love contained within them,
not their rhyme,
Which more fortunate poets will have the skill to
do better.
Just please grant me this loving thought:
"If my friend's inspiration was still in existence
today,
He would have written better poems than these,
To equal the poems written by those with better
equipment.
But since he is dead and poets today are better,
I'll read theirs for the style, and his for his
love."

Sonnet XXXIII

Full many a glorious morning have I seen
Flatter the mountain-tops with sovereign eye,
Kissing with golden face the meadows green,
Gilding pale streams with heavenly alchemy;
Anon permit the basest clouds to ride
With ugly rack on his celestial face,
And from the forlorn world his visage hide,
Stealing unseen to west with this disgrace:
Even so my sun one early morn did shine
With all triumphant splendor on my brow;
But out, alack! he was but one hour mine;
The region cloud hath mask'd him from me now.
Yet him for this my love no whit disdaineth;
Suns of the world may stain when heaven's sun
staineth.

I've seen many glorious mornings when the full sun
Makes the mountains look beautiful under its excellent eye,
And kisses the green meadows with its golden face,
And turns the pale streams gold using divine magic,
Only to permit the most unworthy clouds
To cross its heavenly face,
Hiding it from the wretched world,
Then creeping away unseen to the west in disgrace.
Just like this my sun shone one morning
In triumphant brilliance upon my face,
But—too bad!—he was only mine for an hour,
And the clouds have hidden him from me now.
Still, my love is not corrupt because of this.
Men who are like the sun can disgrace themselves like it does.

Sonnet XXXIV

Why didst thou promise such a beauteous day,
And make me travel forth without my cloak,
To let base clouds o'ertake me in my way,
Hiding thy bravery in their rotten smoke?
'Tis not enough that through the cloud thou break,
To dry the rain on my storm-beaten face,
For no man well of such a salve can speak
That heals the wound and cures not the disgrace:
Nor can thy shame give physic to my grief;
Though thou repent, yet I have still the loss:
The offender's sorrow lends but weak relief
To him that bears the strong offence's cross.
Ah! but those tears are pearl which thy love sheds,
And they are rich and ransom all ill deeds.

Why did you promise such a beautiful day,
And cause me to go out without my coat,
Only to let dark clouds overtake me on the way,
Hiding your splendor in their corrupt mist?
It's not enough that you broke through the clouds
To dry the rain from my storm-beaten face,
Because no man can speak highly of a remedy
That heals the wound but does nothing for the disgrace.
Your sense of shame does not heal my grief—
Even though you are sorry, I still have the loss:
The offender's sorrow offers little relief
To the one who suffers the damage.
Oh, but those tears you shed out of love are like pearls—
They are great and make up for all bad deeds.

Sonnet XXXV

No more be grieved at that which thou hast done:
Roses have thorns, and silver fountains mud;
Clouds and eclipses stain both moon and sun,
And loathsome canker lives in sweetest bud.
All men make faults, and even I in this,
Authorizing thy trespass with compare,
Myself corrupting, salving thy amiss,
Excusing thy sins more than thy sins are;
For to thy sensual fault I bring in sense--
Thy adverse party is thy advocate--
And 'gainst myself a lawful plea commence:
Such civil war is in my love and hate
That I an accessary needs must be
To that sweet thief which sourly robs from me.

Don't be distressed at what you have done:
Roses have thorns, and silver fountains have mud.
Clouds and eclipses sometimes block the moon and sun,
And disgusting worms live in the sweetest flower buds.
Everyone has a fault, and even I, by
Approving of your wrongs by using comparisons
Am reducing and wrongly accounting for and
Excusing your sins more than the sins themselves require.
I am bringing the power of reason to your physical faults—
And thus making the one you have wronged your advocate—
By making a justifiable argument against myself.
I am so at war within myself between love and hate,
That it's necessary to make myself a helper
To the sweet thief who so painfully robs me.

Sonnet XXXVI

Let me confess that we two must be twain,
Although our undivided loves are one:
So shall those blots that do with me remain
Without thy help by me be borne alone.
In our two loves there is but one respect,
Though in our lives a separable spite,
Which though it alter not love's sole effect,
Yet doth it steal sweet hours from love's delight.
I may not evermore acknowledge thee,
Lest my bewailed guilt should do thee shame,
Nor thou with public kindness honour me,
Unless thou take that honour from thy name:
But do not so; I love thee in such sort
As, thou being mine, mine is thy good report.

I have to say that the two of us must separate,
Even though our undivided love is like one:
Our disgraces will stay with me
And without your help, I will carry them alone.
In our two loves there is only one consideration,
But in our lives, despite everything, we must
separate.
Still, it does not alter the love
So much as it steals away the time we can spend
together.
I can not greet you when we meet,
For fear that my regretful guilt will embarrass
you,
And you should not be polite to me either,
Because it will tarnish your good name.
Don't do that. I love you so much
That I value your good reputation as if it were
my own.

Sonnet XXXVII

As a decrepit father takes delight
To see his active child do deeds of youth,
So I, made lame by fortune's dearest spite,
Take all my comfort of thy worth and truth.
For whether beauty, birth, or wealth, or wit,
Or any of these all, or all, or more,
Entitled in thy parts do crowned sit,
I make my love engrafted to this store:
So then I am not lame, poor, nor despised,
Whilst that this shadow doth such substance give
That I in thy abundance am sufficed
And by a part of all thy glory live.
Look, what is best, that best I wish in thee:
This wish I have; then ten times happy me!

Just like an elderly father enjoys
Watching his active child do youthful things,
I too, being lame in my misfortune,
Take comfort in your worth and truth.
Whether it is beauty, birth, wealth or intelligence,
Or any of these, or all of them, or more,
That you are entitled to and invested with,
I attach my love to the fortune.
Then I am not so lame, poor and despised.
As long as this illusion seems real,
Then I have enough in your abundance,
And I live a little in your magnificence.
Whatever is best, I wish that for you:
If I have this wish, then I am ten times happier.

Sonnet XXXVIII

How can my Muse want subject to invent,
While thou dost breathe, that pour'st into my
verse
Thine own sweet argument, too excellent
For every vulgar paper to rehearse?
O, give thyself the thanks, if aught in me
Worthy perusal stand against thy sight;
For who's so dumb that cannot write to thee,
When thou thyself dost give invention light?
Be thou the tenth Muse, ten times more in worth
Than those old nine which rhymers invocate;
And he that calls on thee, let him bring forth
Eternal numbers to outlive long date.
If my slight Muse do please these curious days,
The pain be mine, but thine shall be the praise.

How could I ever lack a subject to write about,
When as long as you live, you pour into my
words,
A sweet subject too excellent
To be written about on ordinary paper?
You can thank yourself if you see anything in my
Examination of you that is worthy in your eyes.
Who could be so wordless they could not write
about you,
When you yourself give light to imagination?
You are the tenth Muse, worth ten times more
Than the other nine which poets call upon.
Let whomever calls on you write
Eternal lines to outlive the end of time.
If my creative work satisfies the hard to please
these days,
The pain of writing will be mine, but you will
have the praise.

Sonnet XXXIX

O, how thy worth with manners may I sing,
When thou art all the better part of me?
What can mine own praise to mine own self bring?
And what is 't but mine own when I praise thee?
Even for this let us divided live,
And our dear love lose name of single one,
That by this separation I may give
That due to thee which thou deservest alone.
O absence, what a torment wouldst thou prove,
Were it not thy sour leisure gave sweet leave
To entertain the time with thoughts of love,
Which time and thoughts so sweetly doth deceive,
And that thou teachest how to make one twain,
By praising him here who doth hence remain!

How can I praise the worth of your character,
When you are the better half of me?
How can I praise you without praising myself?
And what else is it but praise for myself when I praise you?
Because of this, let us live apart,
And our dear love will not be of a single name,
And through the separation I can give you
The honor that you alone deserve.
Oh, absence—you would be such a torment,
If your painful moments did not permit me
To fill the time with thoughts of love,
So that time and my thoughts do sweetly deceive,
And you teach me how to make one into two,
By praising the one who does not remain here!

Sonnet XL

Take all my loves, my love, yea, take them all;
What hast thou then more than thou hadst
before?
No love, my love, that thou mayst true love call;
All mine was thine before thou hadst this more.
Then if for my love thou my love receivest,
I cannot blame thee for my love thou usest;
But yet be blamed, if thou thyself deceivest
By wilful taste of what thyself refusest.
I do forgive thy robbery, gentle thief,
Although thou steal thee all my poverty;
And yet, love knows, it is a greater grief
To bear love's wrong than hate's known injury.
Lascivious grace, in whom all ill well shows,
Kill me with spites; yet we must not be foes.

*Take all of my loves, my love, yes—take them
all.*
*What do you have more of now than you had
before?*
*You have no love, my love, that you can call true
love.*
*All of my love was yours before you had this
little bit more.*
So, if because of my love you receive love,
I can not blame you for the love you've used.
Still, you should be blamed, if you deceive
*By deliberately testing what you have refused
from me.*
I will forgive your stealing from me, gentle thief,
Even thought you are taking the little I have.
And still, love knows, it causes more pain
*To be hurt by a lover than by someone who
hates us.*
Love is graceful even when it looks bad:
*You can kill me with hate, but we will not be
enemies.*

Sonnet XLI

Those petty wrongs that liberty commits,
When I am sometime absent from thy heart,
Thy beauty and thy years full well befits,
For still temptation follows where thou art.
Gentle thou art and therefore to be won,
Beauteous thou art, therefore to be assailed;
And when a woman woos, what woman's son
Will sourly leave her till she have prevailed?
Ay me! but yet thou mightest my seat forbear,
And chide try beauty and thy straying youth,
Who lead thee in their riot even there
Where thou art forced to break a twofold truth,
Hers by thy beauty tempting her to thee,
Thine, by thy beauty being false to me.

Those little slights that freedom allows you
When I am absent from your heart sometimes,
Suit your beauty and youthful age well.
Temptation goes wherever you are.
You are gentle and so you make a nice prize,
And you are good looking and will be pursued.
And when a woman flirts with you, how could you
Possibly ignore her until she has won you over?
Oh, me! But still, please leave my own situation alone,
And please try to keep your beauty and footloose youth in line,
Although your excess may lead you to my mistress,
Where you would break two promises:
Hers to me by tempting her to you with your beauty,
Yours to me by allowing your beauty to win her.

Sonnet XLII

That thou hast her, it is not all my grief,
And yet it may be said I loved her dearly;
That she hath thee, is of my wailing chief,
A loss in love that touches me more nearly.
Loving offenders, thus I will excuse ye:
Thou dost love her, because thou knowst I love her;
And for my sake even so doth she abuse me,
Suffering my friend for my sake to approve her.
If I lose thee, my loss is my love's gain,
And losing her, my friend hath found that loss;
Both find each other, and I lose both twain,
And both for my sake lay on me this cross:
But here's the joy; my friend and I are one;
Sweet flattery! then she loves but me alone.

You have her, but that is not the cause of my sorrows,
Although it can be said I loved her dearly.
That she has you is what's making me miserable,
And that loss of love touches me deeper.
You are both loving in your wrong and so I will excuse you.
You only love her because you know I love her.
And for my sake, she deceives me,
And puts up with you, my friend.
If I lose you, my loss is her gain.
And if I lose her, my friend has gained her.
Both find each other, and I lose both together.
And both of you cause me to feel so much pain.
But here's the happy part: my friend and I are one,
So, there! Because of that, she only loves me.

Sonnet XLIII

When most I wink, then do mine eyes best see,
For all the day they view things unrespected;
But when I sleep, in dreams they look on thee,
And darkly bright are bright in dark directed.
Then thou, whose shadow shadows doth make bright,
How would thy shadow's form form happy show
To the clear day with thy much clearer light,
When to unseeing eyes thy shade shines so!
How would, I say, mine eyes be blessed made
By looking on thee in the living day,
When in dead night thy fair imperfect shade
Through heavy sleep on sightless eyes doth stay!
All days are nights to see till I see thee,
And nights bright days when dreams do show thee me.

When I blink a lot, then my eyes feel better
After viewing things of little value all day.
But when I sleep, it's you I see in my dreams,
And when my eyes find you, they shimmer brightly in the dark.
Then your shadow, which makes even shadows seem brighter,
Can be seen easily and makes for a happy sight.
In the clear day with much clearer light—
When even the blind would see it—your shadow shines.
Oh, can't you see, my eyes would be so brightly blessed,
To look on you in broad daylight?
Still, in the dead of night, your imperfect image
Stays on the inside of my eyelids during my deepest slumber.
All days are night until I see you again,
And nights are brighter than day when I see you in my dreams.

Sonnet XLIV

If the dull substance of my flesh were thought,
Injurious distance should not stop my way;
For then despite of space I would be brought,
From limits far remote where thou dost stay.
No matter then although my foot did stand
Upon the farthest earth removed from thee;
For nimble thought can jump both sea and land
As soon as think the place where he would be.
But ah! thought kills me that I am not thought,
To leap large lengths of miles when thou art
gone,
But that so much of earth and water wrought
I must attend time's leisure with my moan,
Receiving nought by elements so slow
But heavy tears, badges of either's woe.

If the dull substance of my flesh were thought,
Then the great distance to you would not stop
me.
Then, despite the space between us, I would be
brought
From where I am to the far place where you
stay.
It would not matter that my foot rests
On the farthest land from you,
Because nimble thought could jump both sea
and land
As soon as I thought of the place where you
would be.
But, oh! The thought that I am not thought kills
me!
And I am not able to leap large lengths of miles
when you are gone.
There is so much earth and water placed
between us.
I groan and tolerate the slow passing of time,
And receive nothing from elements that are
sluggish,
Except heavy tears, which are proof of my great
sadness.

Sonnet XLV

The other two, slight air and purging fire,
Are both with thee, wherever I abide;
The first my thought, the other my desire,
These present-absent with swift motion slide.
For when these quicker elements are gone
In tender embassy of love to thee,
My life, being made of four, with two alone
Sinks down to death, oppress'd with
melancholy;
Until life's composition be recured
By those swift messengers return'd from thee,
Who even but now come back again, assured
Of thy fair health, recounting it to me:
This told, I joy; but then no longer glad,
I send them back again and straight grow sad.

The other two elements—light air and cleansing air—
Are both with you wherever I am.
Air represents my thoughts and fire represents my desire.
They move between present and absent with a swift motion glide.
When these quick elements are not with me,
They are sending a sweet message of love to you.
My life usually consists of four elements, and when left to only two
I sink almost to death with the weight of depression
Until the proper state of being is restored.
When those swift messengers have returned from you,
And come back again to assure me
Of your good health as they describe it to me,
I am happy to hear it, until I'm not happy again,
And then I send them right back to you and grow depressed.

Sonnet XLVI

Mine eye and heart are at a mortal war
How to divide the conquest of thy sight;
Mine eye my heart thy picture's sight would bar,
My heart mine eye the freedom of that right.
My heart doth plead that thou in him dost lie--
A closet never pierced with crystal eyes—
But the defendant doth that plea deny
And says in him thy fair appearance lies.
To 'cide this title is impanneled
A quest of thoughts, all tenants to the heart,
And by their verdict is determined
The clear eye's moiety and the dear heart's part:
As thus; mine eye's due is thy outward part,
And my heart's right thy inward love of heart.

My eye and my heart are at war with one another
About how to divide the rights to your image.
My eye wants to block your image from my heart,
And my heart wants to block the eye's right to your image.
My heart claims that that your image lies inside of him—
Inside a closet never viewed with glittering eyes—
But my eye plays the defendant and denies this,
Saying that only in him does your beautiful image lie.
To decide who gets the right a court has been assembled,
And my thoughts serve as jurors, although they are loyal to the heart.
They have determined a verdict regarding
The clear eye's portion and the dear heart's part:
So it is that my eye is due the appearance of you
And my heart has the right to what is within your heart.

Sonnet XLVII

Betwixt mine eye and heart a league is took,
And each doth good turns now unto the other:
When that mine eye is famish'd for a look,
Or heart in love with sighs himself doth
smother,
With my love's picture then my eye doth feast
And to the painted banquet bids my heart;
Another time mine eye is my heart's guest
And in his thoughts of love doth share a part:
So, either by thy picture or my love,
Thyself away art resent still with me;
For thou not farther than my thoughts canst
move,
And I am still with them and they with thee;
Or, if they sleep, thy picture in my sight
Awakes my heart to heart's and eye's delight.

An agreement has been made between my eye and my heart,
And each now does the other favors.
When my eye is hungry for a look at you,
Or my heart sighs heavy, smothering sighs of love,
My eye then feasts upon your picture
And invites my heart to join in and gaze, as well.
Another time, my eye may be the heart's guest,
And listen as he shares his thoughts of love for you.
So, either by your picture or by thoughts of love,
You are still present with me even when you are away.
You are never farther than my thoughts can move,
And I am always with them, and they are always with you.
Or, if they sleep, your picture is in my sight,
And it awakes both my heart and eye to delight.

Sonnet XLVIII

How careful was I, when I took my way,
Each trifle under truest bars to thrust,
That to my use it might unused stay
From hands of falsehood, in sure wards of trust!
But thou, to whom my jewels trifles are,
Most worthy of comfort, now my greatest grief,
Thou, best of dearest and mine only care,
Art left the prey of every vulgar thief.
Thee have I not lock'd up in any chest,
Save where thou art not, though I feel thou art,
Within the gentle closure of my breast,
From whence at pleasure thou mayst come and part;
And even thence thou wilt be stol'n, I fear,
For truth proves thievish for a prize so dear.

How careful I used to be when I traveled
To keep every item I own under sturdy locks
So that it would remain with me when not in use
And not be stolen—they were such good locks!
But you, whom makes my greatest jewels seem like nothing,
And is most worthy of keeping safe, is now my greatest worry.
You are the dearest thing to me and all I care about,
And you are wide open to be taken by any common thief.
I have not locked you up in any chest
Except for where you aren't, although I feel you are:
Within my own chest close to my heart,
Where, as you choose, you may come and go,
And even then you will be stolen, I fear, because
Honest men would become thieves to gain a prize like you.

Sonnet XLIX

Against that time, if ever that time come,
When I shall see thee frown on my defects,
When as thy love hath cast his utmost sum,
Call'd to that audit by advised respects;
Against that time when thou shalt strangely pass
And scarcely greet me with that sun thine eye,
When love, converted from the thing it was,
Shall reasons find of settled gravity,--
Against that time do I ensconce me here
Within the knowledge of mine own desert,
And this my hand against myself uprear,
To guard the lawful reasons on thy part:
To leave poor me thou hast the strength of laws,
Since why to love I can allege no cause.

In anticipation of the time, if ever the time comes,
When I see you frown at my faults,
When your love has played itself out
And you are taking everything about me into account;
In anticipation of that time when we pass as strangers
And you do not greet me with a light in your eye,
When love, changed from the thing it was,
Is reasoned away by maturity and wisdom;
In anticipation of that time I want to firmly establish
My full knowledge of all that I lack.
I raise my hand to give testimony against myself,
And to defend every justifiable reason you will have
To leave pitiful me based on good reasons,
Since I can find no reason at all why you love me.

Sonnet L

How heavy do I journey on the way,
When what I seek, my weary travel's end,
Doth teach that ease and that repose to say
'Thus far the miles are measured from thy friend!'
The beast that bears me, tired with my woe,
Plods dully on, to bear that weight in me,
As if by some instinct the wretch did know
His rider loved not speed, being made from thee:
The bloody spur cannot provoke him on
That sometimes anger thrusts into his hide;
Which heavily he answers with a groan,
More sharp to me than spurring to his side;
For that same groan doth put this in my mind;
My grief lies onward and my joy behind.

I feel so sad as I embark on this journey,
Because where I am heading—my weary journey's end—
Will only give me the leisure and rest to say,
'I'm so many miles away from my friend!'
The horse that bears me is tired of my sadness,
And plods on dully, bearing the weight in me.
As if by some instinct he seems to know
His rider is not in a hurry to get away from you.
The bloody spur I use to drive him on does no good
When I sometimes, in anger, thrust it into his side.
He responds to the thrust with such a groan,
Which is more painful to hear that the spur to his side feels,
Because it is the sound of that groan that makes me realize:
My grief lies ahead of me and my joy, behind.

Sonnet LI

Thus can my love excuse the slow offence
Of my dull bearer when from thee I speed:
From where thou art why should I haste me thence?
Till I return, of posting is no need.
O, what excuse will my poor beast then find,
When swift extremity can seem but slow?
Then should I spur, though mounted on the wind;
In winged speed no motion shall I know:
Then can no horse with my desire keep pace;
Therefore desire of perfect'st love being made,
Shall neigh--no dull flesh--in his fiery race;
But love, for love, thus shall excuse my jade;
Since from thee going he went wilful-slow,
Towards thee I'll run, and give him leave to go.

And so my love for you can forgive the slowness
Of my dull horse when I rode away from you:
I mean, why would I want to leave from where you are in a hurry?
So, until I return, no hurry is necessary.
What excuse will my poor horse find then,
When—no matter how fast it goes—it will seem slow?
I will use the spurs even if it seems to ride the wind.
If it seems to fly, it will not be moving forward fast enough for me.
No horse will be able to keep up with my desire,
Because my desire will be made of perfect love,
And the horse I ride must neigh—without dull flesh—in a fiery race to you.
But my love, out of love, I will excuse my tired horse
Since he went away from you so slowly.
I will run on my own toward you, and let him go free.

Sonnet LII

So am I as the rich, whose blessed key
Can bring him to his sweet up-locked treasure,
The which he will not every hour survey,
For blunting the fine point of seldom pleasure.
Therefore are feasts so solemn and so rare,
Since, seldom coming, in the long year set,
Like stones of worth they thinly placed are,
Or captain jewels in the carcanet.
So is the time that keeps you as my chest,
Or as the wardrobe which the robe doth hide,
To make some special instant special blest,
By new unfolding his imprison'd pride.
Blessed are you, whose worthiness gives scope,
Being had, to triumph, being lack'd, to hope.

So, I'm like the wealthy man, whose blessed key
Can bring him to his sweet locked-up treasure,
Which he will resist looking at every hour,
Because it will dull the pleasure when he looks
at it.
So, the feasts of looking are formal and rare,
Since, as they come so infrequently, they are set
in the year
Like stones of value are just barely placed,
Like the main jewels set in a necklace.
In the same way, the time that keeps you away
from me is a chest
Or a wardrobe that holds the robe in which you
hide,
Making some small moment especially blessed,
When it unfolds to reveal what has been
contained within.
You are blessed with a great worth that ranges
wide:
Those who have you feel triumphant, while
others hope to have you.

Sonnet LIII

What is your substance, whereof are you made,
That millions of strange shadows on you tend?
Since every one hath, every one, one shade,
And you, but one, can every shadow lend.
Describe Adonis, and the counterfeit
Is poorly imitated after you;
On Helen's cheek all art of beauty set,
And you in Grecian tires are painted new:
Speak of the spring and foison of the year;
The one doth shadow of your beauty show,
The other as your bounty doth appear;
And you in every blessed shape we know.
In all external grace you have some part,
But you like none, none you, for constant heart.

What are you made of—of what substance?
That millions of reflections tend to look like
you?
While everyone has—everyone!—one image,
You seem to look like every image.
Try to paint Adonis, and the painting will be
A poor imitation of you.
And if Helen's cheek and her beauty were
painted,
It would be you again in Greek clothes.
Mention spring and the abundance of fall—
Spring is only a shadow of your beauty,
And fall can not match your great generosity.
We see you in every blessed image we know.
You are like everything beautiful in an image,
But nothing can match the constancy of your
heart.

Sonnet LIV

O, how much more doth beauty beauteous seem
By that sweet ornament which truth doth give!
The rose looks fair, but fairer we it deem
For that sweet odour which doth in it live.
The canker-blooms have full as deep a dye
As the perfumed tincture of the roses,
Hang on such thorns and play as wantonly
When summer's breath their masked buds
discloses:
But, for their virtue only is their show,
They live unwoo'd and unrespected fade,
Die to themselves. Sweet roses do not so;
Of their sweet deaths are sweetest odours made:
And so of you, beauteous and lovely youth,
When that shall fade, my verse distills your
truth.

*Oh, how much more beautiful does beauty
appear,
When its sweetness is matched with truth and
honesty!
The rose looks beautiful, but we say it is more
beautiful
For the sweet scent that it carries.
Wild roses have a full and deep color,
The same as the perfumed roses have.
Their thorns are the same and they display as
playfully
When the warm summer air opens their blooms.
But their only good point is in their appearance,
They live unloved and have little value as they
fade,
And so they die alone. Fragrant roses do not do
this:
As they fade, they produce the sweetest scent
possible.
And so will you, beautiful and lovely youth,
because
When you fade, my verse will hold your essence.*

Sonnet LV

Not marble, nor the gilded monuments
Of princes, shall outlive this powerful rhyme;
But you shall shine more bright in these contents
Than unswept stone besmear'd with sluttish
time.
When wasteful war shall statues overturn,
And broils root out the work of masonry,
Nor Mars his sword nor war's quick fire shall
burn
The living record of your memory.
'Gainst death and all-oblivious enmity
Shall you pace forth; your praise shall still find
room
Even in the eyes of all posterity
That wear this world out to the ending doom.
So, till the judgment that yourself arise,
You live in this, and dwell in lover's eyes.

Neither marble nor the gold-plated monuments
Of princes will outlive this powerful poem,
You will shine more brightly in these lines
Than abandoned stone discolored with filthy
time.
When wasteful wars overturn statues
And battles tear up stonework and floors,
Neither War's fierce sword nor his quick fire
will burn
The living record of your memory.
Avoiding death and forgetful hostility,
You will walk forward and your praise will still
find room
In the eyes of a long line of descendants,
Lasting until the end of the world.
So, until Judgment Day when you are raised
again
You live in this poem and in the eyes of lovers.

Sonnet LVI

Sweet love, renew thy force; be it not said
Thy edge should blunter be than appetite,
Which but to-day by feeding is allay'd,
To-morrow sharpen'd in his former might:
So, love, be thou; although to-day thou fill
Thy hungry eyes even till they wink with
fullness,
To-morrow see again, and do not kill
The spirit of love with a perpetual dullness.
Let this sad interim like the ocean be
Which parts the shore, where two contracted
new
Come daily to the banks, that, when they see
Return of love, more blest may be the view;
Else call it winter, which being full of care
Makes summer's welcome thrice more wish'd,
more rare.

Sweet love, renew your strength. They say
The edge of love is blunter than desire's,
Which is easily satisfied today
Only to be as sharp and strong again tomorrow.
So, love, be like that: although today you look
on your lover
With hungry eyes until you want to close them
because they feel full,
Look again tomorrow, and do not kill
The spirit of love with a constant dullness.
Let this sad break between us be like an ocean
Which parts the shores where two newly
engaged lovers
Come to the banks every day, and when they see
Their love again on the other side, the view is
blessed.
Or let it be like winter, which is so full of trouble
It makes summer three times more welcome and
rare.

Sonnet LVII

Being your slave, what should I do but tend
Upon the hours and times of your desire?
I have no precious time at all to spend,
Nor services to do, till you require.
Nor dare I chide the world-without-end hour
Whilst I, my sovereign, watch the clock for you,
Nor think the bitterness of absence sour
When you have bid your servant once adieu;
Nor dare I question with my jealous thought
Where you may be, or your affairs suppose,
But, like a sad slave, stay and think of nought
Save, where you are how happy you make those.
So true a fool is love that in your will,
Though you do any thing, he thinks no ill.

Since I am your slave, what can I do except attend
To the hours and times of your desire?
I have no precious time of my own to spend at all,
Or services to do, until you require me.
I don't dare to complain about the endless hours
While I wait for you, my king, watching the clock,
Or think about how bitter and sour your absence is
Once you have bid your servant goodbye.
I certainly don't dare to voice my jealous thoughts
About where you might be, or what you are up to,
But, like a sad slave, I wait and think about nothing
Except how happy you must be making someone, wherever you are.
Love makes a person such a loyal fool
That no matter what you do, he won't think badly of you.

Sonnet LVIII

That god forbid that made me first your slave,
I should in thought control your times of
pleasure,
Or at your hand the account of hours to crave,
Being your vassal, bound to stay your leisure!
O, let me suffer, being at your beck,
The imprison'd absence of your liberty;
And patience, tame to sufferance, bide each
cheque,
Without accusing you of injury.
Be where you list, your charter is so strong
That you yourself may privilege your time
To what you will; to you it doth belong
Yourself to pardon of self-doing crime.
I am to wait, though waiting so be hell;
Not blame your pleasure, be it ill or well.

May the god that decided to make me your slave
Never allow me to think about having control
over when you see me,
Or to ask for an accounting of how you spend
your hours.
I am your slave, and so I must wait for you to
decide to see me!
Oh, let me suffer quietly, while being at your
call,
In a prison-like absence while you are free to do
as you please.
Give me the patience to endure and suffer each
rebuke
Without accusing you of hurting me.
You can be where you wish—your privilege is so
strong
That you, yourself, may control your time
And do whatever you want. It is your right
To forgive yourself of any selfish crime.
I am to wait, although waiting is like hell,
And not blame you for doing as you please,
whether it's for bad or good.

Sonnet LIX

If there be nothing new, but that which is
Hath been before, how are our brains beguiled,
Which, labouring for invention, bear amiss
The second burden of a former child!
O, that record could with a backward look,
Even of five hundred courses of the sun,
Show me your image in some antique book,
Since mind at first in character was done!
That I might see what the old world could say
To this composed wonder of your frame;
Whether we are mended, or whether better they,
Or whether revolution be the same.
O, sure I am, the wits of former days
To subjects worse have given admiring praise.

If there is nothing new and if everything that is
Has been before, then our brains are being
tricked
When, working to write something new, we only
Write what has been written before!
Oh, if I could look back over the record
To even five hundred years ago,
I wonder if I'd find the likeness of you in an old
book,
Written when letters were first formed!
Then I could see what the writers in the past
would say
About the beauty of your body,
And whether we write better now, or whether
they did,
Or if it's really just about the same.
I am fairly certain that the poets of olden days
Gave high praise to subjects less deserving than
you.

Sonnet LX

Like as the waves make towards the pebbled shore,
So do our minutes hasten to their end;
Each changing place with that which goes before,
In sequent toil all forwards do contend.
Nativity, once in the main of light,
Crawls to maturity, wherewith being crown'd,
Crooked elipses 'gainst his glory fight,
And Time that gave doth now his gift confound.
Time doth transfix the flourish set on youth
And delves the parallels in beauty's brow,
Feeds on the rarities of nature's truth,
And nothing stands but for his scythe to mow:
And yet to times in hope my verse shall stand,
Praising thy worth, despite his cruel hand.

In the same way waves make their way toward the pebbled shore,
The minutes we have hurry to their end,
Each one changing place with the one before it,
As all work together to move forward in a sequence.
Birth, once in the spotlight,
Crawls toward old age, where—once it is crowned—
Faces a crooked path as it fights its way to glory.
Time, having given its gift, now destroys it.
It sharply pierces the decoration of youth
And digs furrows in beauty's forehead;
It feeds on the exceptional specimens of nature—
Nothing exists that its scythe will not mow down:
Still, it is my hope that my poems will survive
And praise your worth, despite Time's cruel hand.

Sonnet LXI

Is it thy will thy image should keep open
My heavy eyelids to the weary night?
Dost thou desire my slumbers should be broken,
While shadows like to thee do mock my sight?
Is it thy spirit that thou send'st from thee
So far from home into my deeds to pry,
To find out shames and idle hours in me,
The scope and tenor of thy jealousy?
O, no! thy love, though much, is not so great:
It is my love that keeps mine eye awake;
Mine own true love that doth my rest defeat,
To play the watchman ever for thy sake:
For thee watch I whilst thou dost wake
elsewhere,
From me far off, with others all too near.

Is it your intent that your image should keep
My heavy eyelids open during the weary night?
Do you desire me to lose sleep,
While visions of you ridicule me?
Is it your spirit that you send to me
While you are far from home to see what I am
up to?
To find out things I might be embarrased about
during my idle hours?
Is this due to the depth and substance of your
jealousy?
Oh, no. Your love for me, though deep, is not
that deep:
It is my love for you that keeps me awake at
night,
My own true love that will not let me sleep.
I play the constant watchman for your sake:
For you, I watch while you wake somewhere
else
Far away from me, with someone else too near.

Sonnet LXII

Sin of self-love possesseth all mine eye
And all my soul and all my every part;
And for this sin there is no remedy,
It is so grounded inward in my heart.
Methinks no face so gracious is as mine,
No shape so true, no truth of such account;
And for myself mine own worth do define,
As I all other in all worths surmount.
But when my glass shows me myself indeed,
Beated and chopp'd with tann'd antiquity,
Mine own self-love quite contrary I read;
Self so self-loving were iniquity.
'Tis thee, myself, that for myself I praise,
Painting my age with beauty of thy days.

The sin of self-love takes possession of my eyes,
And all of my soul and every part of me.
There is no remedy for this sin—
It is so deeply established in my heart.
I think that no face is so pleasing as mine,
No body so well proportioned, no virtue so
accountable.
And so for myself I define my worth,
Which exceeds the worth of others, by far.
But when I look into my mirror and see
How beaten, broken and aged with time and sun
I am,
My self-love shifts and I feel the opposite:
To love myself would be simply wicked.
It's you I praise when I praise myself,
Beautifying my age with your youth.

Sonnet LXIII

Against my love shall be, as I am now,
With Time's injurious hand crush'd and o'er-
worn;
When hours have drain'd his blood and fill'd his
brow
With lines and wrinkles; when his youthful
morn
Hath travell'd on to age's steepy night,
And all those beauties whereof now he's king
Are vanishing or vanish'd out of sight,
Stealing away the treasure of his spring;
For such a time do I now fortify
Against confounding age's cruel knife,
That he shall never cut from memory
My sweet love's beauty, though my lover's life:
His beauty shall in these black lines be seen,
And they shall live, and he in them still green.

*In anticipation of the time when my love will be
as I am now—
Crushed and worn-out by Time's damaging
hand—
When hours have weakened his blood and filled
his forehead
With lines and wrinkles, and when his youthful
morning
Has traveled into the steep night of old age,
And all of those beauties in which he is now in
command
Are vanishing or have vanished out of sight,
Stealing away the treasure of his youth—
In anticipation of that time I am trying to
strengthen
Him against the destructive edge of age's cruel
knife
So that he will never be cut from memory.
My sweet love's beauty will remain even if time
takes his life:
His beauty will be seen in these black, inked
lines,
And as long as these lines exist, he will remain
young.*

Sonnet LXIV

When I have seen by Time's fell hand defaced
The rich proud cost of outworn buried age;
When sometime lofty towers I see down-razed
And brass eternal slave to mortal rage;
When I have seen the hungry ocean gain
Advantage on the kingdom of the shore,
And the firm soil win of the watery main,
Increasing store with loss and loss with store;
When I have seen such interchange of state,
Or state itself confounded to decay;
Ruin hath taught me thus to ruminate,
That Time will come and take my love away.
This thought is as a death, which cannot choose
But weep to have that which it fears to lose.

Now that I have seen Time's cruel hand
disfigure
The expensive and proud monuments of men
buried long ago;
And now that I have seen high towers torn to the
ground,
And brass that was supposed to be eternal
ruined by human rage;
Now that I have seen the hungry ocean gain
advantage
And overtake the kingdom of the shore,
And firm soil overtake the water,
So that each one's increase is the other's loss;
Now that I have seen everything changing into
something else,
Or being destroyed or left to decay,
I have learned to think about the fact
That Time will come and take my love away.
This thought feels like death, and I cannot help
But weep about what I have and fear to lose.

Sonnet LXV

Since brass, nor stone, nor earth, nor boundless sea,
But sad mortality o'er-sways their power,
How with this rage shall beauty hold a plea,
Whose action is no stronger than a flower?
O, how shall summer's honey breath hold out
Against the wreckful siege of battering days,
When rocks impregnable are not so stout,
Nor gates of steel so strong, but Time decays?
O fearful meditation! where, alack,
Shall Time's best jewel from Time's chest lie hid?
Or what strong hand can hold his swift foot back?
Or who his spoil of beauty can forbid?
O, none, unless this miracle have might,
That in black ink my love may still shine bright.

Since neither brass, nor stone, nor earth, nor boundless seas
Are powerful enough to withstand being taken over by mortality,
How could beauty possibly stand a chance,
When it is no stronger than a flower?
How will the sweet breath of summer hold out
Against the destructive hold of battering days,
When even the hardest rocks are not sturdy enough,
And gates of steel are not strong enough to avoid being decayed by Time?
Oh, these thoughts make me fearful! Where, tell me,
Can Time's best jewel be hidden from Time?
What hand is strong enough to hold back Time?
Who can forbid that he spoil beauty?
No one can, unless by a strong miracle
My love shines bright in these black, inked lines.

Sonnet LXVI

Tired with all these, for restful death I cry,
As, to behold desert a beggar born,
And needy nothing trimm'd in jollity,
And purest faith unhappily forsworn,
And guilded honour shamefully misplaced,
And maiden virtue rudely strumpeted,
And right perfection wrongfully disgraced,
And strength by limping sway disabled,
And art made tongue-tied by authority,
And folly doctor-like controlling skill,
And simple truth miscall'd simplicity,
And captive good attending captain ill:
Tired with all these, from these would I be gone,
Save that, to die, I leave my love alone.

Tired of all of this, I wish for a restful death.
I'm tired of seeing deserving people become
beggars,
And unworthy people dressed up in fine clothes,
And vows made in faith broken,
And gold-plated honors given to shameful
people,
And virtuous maidens violently made into
whores,
And people who are right wrongfully
humiliated,
And the strong disabled by the weak that hold
power,
And art censored by authority,
And fools controlling those with knowledge like
doctors control the ill,
And common sense misnamed as foolishness,
And good held captive to evil.
I am tired of all of this and would go
Except that—if I die—I would have to leave my
love alone.

Sonnet LXVII

Ah! wherefore with infection should he live,
And with his presence grace impiety,
That sin by him advantage should achieve
And lace itself with his society?
Why should false painting imitate his cheek
And steal dead seeing of his living hue?
Why should poor beauty indirectly seek
Roses of shadow, since his rose is true?
Why should he live, now Nature bankrupt is,
Beggar'd of blood to blush through lively veins?
For she hath no exchequer now but his,
And, proud of many, lives upon his gains.
O, him she stores, to show what wealth she had
In days long since, before these last so bad.

Why should he live with rottenness
And grace wickedness with his presence
So that sinners can take advantage of him
And make themselves look better by being in his
company?
Why should inadequate portrait painters paint
his likeness
And steal lifeless images of his living
complexion?
Why should those not as beautiful as him seek
To be images of a rose, when he is the authentic
rose?
And why should he live, now that Nature is so
spent
That she has to beg for blood to blush living
veins?
She has no resources now except for his,
And—swelling with the many she needs to
provide for—she borrows his gains.
Oh, she keeps him in store to show what wealth
she once had
In days long gone, before these recent bad days
arrived.

Sonnet LXVIII

Thus is his cheek the map of days outworn,
When beauty lived and died as flowers do now,
Before the bastard signs of fair were born,
Or durst inhabit on a living brow;
Before the golden tresses of the dead,
The right of sepulchres, were shorn away,
To live a second life on second head;
Ere beauty's dead fleece made another gay:
In him those holy antique hours are seen,
Without all ornament, itself and true,
Making no summer of another's green,
Robbing no old to dress his beauty new;
And him as for a map doth Nature store,
To show false Art what beauty was of yore.

So, in his face is the image of how things were in former days,
When beauty lived and died as easily as flowers do now.
This was before the inferior signs of beauty originated,
And before they inhabited a living forehead.
This was before the golden hair of the dead,
Which rightfully belongs in the grave, was cut off
To live again on another head.
It was before beauty's dead hair made another pretty.
In him, those sacred old days can be seen
Without uneccesary decoration—authentic and true—
Not taking another's youth to look youthful,
And not robbing from the old to make his beauty new.
Nature keeps his image in storage
So she can show false Art what beauty used to be.

Sonnet LXIX

Those parts of thee that the world's eye doth view	*Those parts of you that can readily be seen by the world,*
Want nothing that the thought of hearts can mend;	*Lack nothing, and no one has thoughts of improving on them.*
All tongues, the voice of souls, give thee that due,	*Everyone speaks highly and gives those parts of you praise,*
Uttering bare truth, even so as foes commend.	*And tell the truth; even your enemies compliment your good looks.*
Thy outward thus with outward praise is crown'd;	*So, your outward appearance is thus crowned with outward praise,*
But those same tongues that give thee so thine own	*But those same people that give you that praise*
In other accents do this praise confound	*Talk in other tones that destroy it*
By seeing farther than the eye hath shown.	*When they look beyond what only the eye can see.*
They look into the beauty of thy mind,	*They look into the beauty of your mind,*
And that, in guess, they measure by thy deeds;	*Which they guess at by summing up your actions;*
Then, churls, their thoughts, although their eyes were kind,	*Then, the villains, after giving kind praise to your looks,*
To thy fair flower add the rank smell of weeds:	*Add words that are like the rank smell of weeds on a flower:*
But why thy odour matcheth not thy show,	*The reason the foul scent does not match your appearance*
The solve is this, that thou dost common grow.	*Is that you are becoming cheap and vulgar.*

Sonnet LXX

That thou art blamed shall not be thy defect,
For slander's mark was ever yet the fair;
The ornament of beauty is suspect,
A crow that flies in heaven's sweetest air.
So thou be good, slander doth but approve
Thy worth the greater, being woo'd of time;
For canker vice the sweetest buds doth love,
And thou present'st a pure unstained prime.
Thou hast pass'd by the ambush of young days,
Either not assail'd or victor being charged;
Yet this thy praise cannot be so thy praise,
To tie up envy evermore enlarged:
If some suspect of ill mask'd not thy show,
Then thou alone kingdoms of hearts shouldst owe.

People blame you for things that will not be your fault
Because the beautiful always carry the mark of slander.
The person who is beautiful is always suspected of wrong—
A dark crow that flies in the sweetest air of heaven.
As long as you are good, slander will confirm
Your worth all the more, and it is courted by time.
Vice, like a parasite, loves the sweetest buds most,
And you present as pure and unblemished in your prime.
You have evaded the ambush in your younger days,
Because you either were not attacked, or you proved your innocence, once charged;
Still, this praise I give you cannot be enough praise
To keep the envy of others from always growing:
If some suspicion of evil did not mask your appearance,
Then you alone would have a kingdom of hearts in love with you.

Sonnet LXXI

No longer mourn for me when I am dead
Then you shall hear the surly sullen bell
Give warning to the world that I am fled
From this vile world, with vilest worms to dwell:
Nay, if you read this line, remember not
The hand that writ it; for I love you so
That I in your sweet thoughts would be forgot
If thinking on me then should make you woe.
O, if, I say, you look upon this verse
When I perhaps compounded am with clay,
Do not so much as my poor name rehearse.
But let your love even with my life decay,
Lest the wise world should look into your moan
And mock you with me after I am gone.

Do not mourn for me when I am dead any longer
Than you hear the funeral bell
Ringing my passing, announcing to the word that I am gone
From this vile world to live with the vilest worms.
No, if you read this line, don't remember
The hand that wrote it, because I love you so much
That I would want your sweet thoughts to forget me,
If thinking about me would make you sad.
Oh, if, say, you should look at this poem
When I am combined with the clay of the earth,
Do not even say my poor name out loud.
Let your love fade away as my life did,
Otherwise, the world might look at you in your grief
And ridicule you for missing me after I am gone.

Sonnet LXXII

O, lest the world should task you to recite
What merit lived in me, that you should love
After my death, dear love, forget me quite,
For you in me can nothing worthy prove;
Unless you would devise some virtuous lie,
To do more for me than mine own desert,
And hang more praise upon deceased I
Than niggard truth would willingly impart:
O, lest your true love may seem false in this,
That you for love speak well of me untrue,
My name be buried where my body is,
And live no more to shame nor me nor you.
For I am shamed by that which I bring forth,
And so should you, to love things nothing worth.

Oh, should the world ask you to say
What good lived in me that makes you love
Me after my death, dear love, forget me entirely,
Because there is nothing in me that is worthy,
Unless you come up with some virtuous lie,
That gives me more than I deserve,
And hangs more praise on the dead me
Than any unwilling truth would actually give;
Oh, because your true love may seem false in this—
That you speak well of me because of love—
Just bury my name with my body,
And let me lie dead and no longer bring shame to you or me.
I am shamed by what I bring forth,
And you should be, too, to love things worth nothing.

Sonnet LXXIII

That time of year thou mayst in me behold
When yellow leaves, or none, or few, do hang
Upon those boughs which shake against the cold,
Bare ruin'd choirs, where late the sweet birds sang.
In me thou seest the twilight of such day
As after sunset fadeth in the west,
Which by and by black night doth take away,
Death's second self, that seals up all in rest.
In me thou see'st the glowing of such fire
That on the ashes of his youth doth lie,
As the death-bed whereon it must expire
Consumed with that which it was nourish'd by.
This thou perceivest, which makes thy love more strong,
To love that well which thou must leave ere long.

You may see in me that time of year
When yellow leaves, or none, or few, still hang
Upon the limbs that shake against the cold—
Bare ruined choirs where until recently sweet birds sang.
In me you may see the twilight of the day
That fades in the west after sunset,
Which, by and by, the black night takes away,
Like Death's twin, sealing everyone in sleep.
You see in me the glow of a fire
That lies on the ashes of its youth,
As the death-bed on which it must die
Is consumed with what nourished it the most.
You see all of this, and it makes your love stronger,
Since we love most what we know will leave us soon.

Sonnet LXXIV

But be contented: when that fell arrest
Without all bail shall carry me away,
My life hath in this line some interest,
Which for memorial still with thee shall stay.
When thou reviewest this, thou dost review
The very part was consecrate to thee:
The earth can have but earth, which is his due;
My spirit is thine, the better part of me:
So then thou hast but lost the dregs of life,
The prey of worms, my body being dead,
The coward conquest of a wretch's knife,
Too base of thee to be remembered.
The worth of that is that which it contains,
And that is this, and this with thee remains.

Try to be calm: when that deadly arrest
Carries me away without any bail,
There is some of my life in these lines,
Which will remain as a memorial for you.
When you look over this, you will see
The part that was dedicated to you.
The earth can have what is earthly, which is its
due,
But my spirit is yours, which is the better part of
me.
When I am gone, you will have the last dregs of
my life—
The food of worms, my dead body,
The only part cowardly enough to be killed by a
knife,
And too worthless to be remembered.
The worth of it is what it contains,
And that is this, and this remains with you.

Sonnet LXXV

So are you to my thoughts as food to life,
Or as sweet-season'd showers are to the ground;
And for the peace of you I hold such strife
As 'twixt a miser and his wealth is found;
Now proud as an enjoyer and anon
Doubting the filching age will steal his treasure,
Now counting best to be with you alone,
Then better'd that the world may see my
pleasure;
Sometime all full with feasting on your sight
And by and by clean starved for a look;
Possessing or pursuing no delight,
Save what is had or must from you be took.
Thus do I pine and surfeit day by day,
Or gluttoning on all, or all away.

You in my thoughts is like food to the living,
Or like much needed showers to the ground,
And to get the peace you give me I struggle
In the same way a miser does with his wealth;
One moment I am proud to be enjoying you and
the next
I am full of doubt that someone will steal my
treasure,
Then I am figuring it would be best to be alone
with you,
And then I think it would be better if the world
saw my pleasure.
Sometimes I am full with feasting on the sight of
you
And then, by and by, I am completely starved for
a glance.
Possessing you or pursuing you holds no
delight,
Except for what is to be had or must be taken
from you.
And so I long for you or over-indulge day by
day:
I either feast on all of you, or none at all.

Sonnet LXXVI

Why is my verse so barren of new pride,
So far from variation or quick change?
Why with the time do I not glance aside
To new-found methods and to compounds strange?
Why write I still all one, ever the same,
And keep invention in a noted weed,
That every word doth almost tell my name,
Showing their birth and where they did proceed?
O, know, sweet love, I always write of you,
And you and love are still my argument;
So all my best is dressing old words new,
Spending again what is already spent:
For as the sun is daily new and old,
So is my love still telling what is told.

Why are my poems so lacking of new qualities,
And so set on not having variation or lively change?
Why don't I look to the times and glance at
The newfound methods and startling constructions?
Why do I still write the same as ever,
And keep my writing in a familiar style,
So that every word practically mentions my name,
Showing its birth and how it came into being?
Oh, sweet love, I always write about you,
And you and love are still my subject.
So, at my best, I am dressing old words in new clothes,
Spending again what has already been spent,
Just like the sun is every day new and old,
My love for you keeps wanting to tell what is told.

Sonnet LXXVII

Thy glass will show thee how thy beauties wear,
Thy dial how thy precious minutes waste;
The vacant leaves thy mind's imprint will bear,
And of this book this learning mayst thou taste.
The wrinkles which thy glass will truly show
Of mouthed graves will give thee memory;
Thou by thy dial's shady stealth mayst know
Time's thievish progress to eternity.
Look, what thy memory can not contain
Commit to these waste blanks, and thou shalt find
Those children nursed, deliver'd from thy brain,
To take a new acquaintance of thy mind.
These offices, so oft as thou wilt look,
Shall profit thee and much enrich thy book.

The mirror will reveal how your beauty wears;
The clock will show you the precious minutes you waste;
The blank pages will bear your mind's thoughts,
And by keeping this book you will learn some things:
The wrinkles you see that the mirror truly shows
Will remind you of open-mouthed graves;
You will learn from the stealthy passing of the clock's hands
About how Time steals away to eternity.
Look: what you cannot remember
Write it down on these blank pages and you will find
These infant thoughts nursed once delivered from your brain.
They will be like new acquaintances to your mind when you see them again.
Performing these tasks, as long as you attend to them,
Will serve you well and will enrich your book.

Sonnet LXXVIII

So oft have I invoked thee for my Muse
And found such fair assistance in my verse
As every alien pen hath got my use
And under thee their poesy disperse.
Thine eyes that taught the dumb on high to sing
And heavy ignorance aloft to fly
Have added feathers to the learned's wing
And given grace a double majesty.
Yet be most proud of that which I compile,
Whose influence is thine and born of thee:
In others' works thou dost but mend the style,
And arts with thy sweet graces graced be;
But thou art all my art and dost advance
As high as learning my rude ignorance.

I have so often named you as my Muse,
And you've assisted my poetry so much,
That other writers have used you, too,
And now they scatter their poetry in your name.
Your eyes that have taught the speechless to sing
on high,
And lifted the ignorant until they can fly.
It has added feathers to intelligent wings,
And have doubled the majesty of the graceful.
Yet you should be most proud of what I
compose,
Since its sole influence is yours and born of you:
In others' works you only improve the style,
And grace their arts with your sweet graces;
But you are all of my art and you lift
My crude ignorance into intelligence.

Sonnet LXXIX

Whilst I alone did call upon thy aid,
My verse alone had all thy gentle grace,
But now my gracious numbers are decay'd
And my sick Muse doth give another place.
I grant, sweet love, thy lovely argument
Deserves the travail of a worthier pen,
Yet what of thee thy poet doth invent
He robs thee of and pays it thee again.
He lends thee virtue and he stole that word
From thy behavior; beauty doth he give
And found it in thy cheek; he can afford
No praise to thee but what in thee doth live.
Then thank him not for that which he doth say,
Since what he owes thee thou thyself dost pay.

When I was the only one who called upon you to aid my poems,
My poems were the only ones that contained your gentle grace;
But now my blessed numbers are lessened,
And my sick Muse forces me to allow another take my place.
I admit, sweet love, that such a sweet subject as you
Deserves the labor of a worthier pen;
Yet whatever the poet invents about you,
He steals it from you and pays it to you again.
If he writes about your virtue, he stole that word
By watching you behavior; if he names beauty,
He found it in your face. He cannot afford
To give you any praise but what he finds in you.
So don't thank him for what he says about you,
Since you are paying him what he owes to you.

Sonnet LXXX

O, how I faint when I of you do write,
Knowing a better spirit doth use your name,
And in the praise thereof spends all his might,
To make me tongue-tied, speaking of your fame!
But since your worth, wide as the ocean is,
The humble as the proudest sail doth bear,
My saucy bark inferior far to his
On your broad main doth wilfully appear.
Your shallowest help will hold me up afloat,
Whilst he upon your soundless deep doth ride;
Or being wreck'd, I am a worthless boat,
He of tall building and of goodly pride:
Then if he thrive and I be cast away,
The worst was this; my love was my decay.

Oh, how fearful I feel when I write about you,
Knowing a better poet uses your name,
And spends all of his strength in praising you,
And it makes me feel tongue-tied, trying to describe you!
But since your worth is as wide as the ocean,
The humble and the proudest can both sail it.
So even though my defiant ship is very inferior to his,
On your broad ocean I do deliberately appear.
Your shallowest waters will keep me afloat,
While he rides upon your deepest depths;
If I am wrecked, I am just a worthless boat,
While his is tall as a building and something to be proud of:
So if he thrives and I am cast away,
The worst of it will be that my love for you was the cause of my ruin.

Sonnet LXXXI

Or I shall live your epitaph to make,
Or you survive when I in earth am rotten;
From hence your memory death cannot take,
Although in me each part will be forgotten.
Your name from hence immortal life shall have,
Though I, once gone, to all the world must die:
The earth can yield me but a common grave,
When you entombed in men's eyes shall lie.
Your monument shall be my gentle verse,
Which eyes not yet created shall o'er-read,
And tongues to be your being shall rehearse
When all the breathers of this world are dead;
You still shall live--such virtue hath my pen--
Where breath most breathes, even in the mouths
of men.

I may outlive you to write your epitaph,
Or you may survive me when I am in the earth
rotting:
Death cannot take your memory away,
Although it will cause my part to be forgotten.
Your name will have immortal life,
Even though I, once gone, will be dead to the
world.
The earth will give me a common grave,
While you will be entombed for all mens' eyes to
see.
Your monument will be my gentle poems,
Which the eyes of those not yet born will read,
And tongues to come will talk about your
essence,
When all those who breathe now are dead;
You will still live—that is the virtue of my pen—
In the place where life is: in the breath in the
mouths of men.

Sonnet LXXXII

I grant thou wert not married to my Muse
And therefore mayst without attaint o'erlook
The dedicated words which writers use
Of their fair subject, blessing every book
Thou art as fair in knowledge as in hue,
Finding thy worth a limit past my praise,
And therefore art enforced to seek anew
Some fresher stamp of the time-bettering days
And do so, love; yet when they have devised
What strained touches rhetoric can lend,
Thou truly fair wert truly sympathized
In true plain words by thy true-telling friend;
And their gross painting might be better used
Where cheeks need blood; in thee it is abused.

I admit you are not married to my poetry,
And so you may look without doing wrong
At the words other writers have written
About you, their fair subject, who blesses every
book,
Since you are as knowledgeable as your
complexion is beautiful,
And you will find your worth is just beyond my
praise,
And so you will be forced to seek a newer
And fresher account written in the style of the
times.
So go ahead and do so, love, and yet when they
have created
Whatever they can with a strained touch of
modern rhetoric,
Know that you were truly matched
With a friend who could tell the truth about you
in plain words;
The other poets' extreme methods might be of
more use
Where color is needed in cheeks: to use it for
you would be wrong.

Sonnet LXXXIII

I never saw that you did painting need
And therefore to your fair no painting set;
I found, or thought I found, you did exceed
The barren tender of a poet's debt;
And therefore have I slept in your report,
That you yourself being extant well might show
How far a modern quill doth come too short,
Speaking of worth, what worth in you doth grow.
This silence for my sin you did impute,
Which shall be most my glory, being dumb;
For I impair not beauty being mute,
When others would give life and bring a tomb.
There lives more life in one of your fair eyes
Than both your poets can in praise devise.

I never saw that you required beautifying,
And so I did not try to beautify your beauty;
I saw, or thought I saw, that you exceed
The empty words of a poet's obligation;
And, because of this, I paid no attention to the description
That you yourself, being in existence, will show.
A modern pen will come up too short,
When speaking of your worth, and the worth that grows in you.
You called me to account for my silence in this regard,
Even though I feel my silence is my brilliance—
I do not dishonor your beauty by being silent.
Others bring you to life while burying you.
More life exists in one of your beautiful eyes
Than both of your poets could ever begin to describe.

Sonnet LXXXIV

Who is it that says most? which can say more
Than this rich praise, that you alone are you?
In whose confine immured is the store
Which should example where your equal grew.
Lean penury within that pen doth dwell
That to his subject lends not some small glory;
But he that writes of you, if he can tell
That you are you, so dignifies his story,
Let him but copy what in you is writ,
Not making worse what nature made so clear,
And such a counterpart shall fame his wit,
Making his style admired every where.
You to your beauteous blessings add a curse,
Being fond on praise, which makes your praises
worse.

Which poet says the most? Which can say more
Than to give the rich praise that you alone are
you?
In whose domain is the treasure confined
Which is the example of what you equal?
A poverty-stricken writer will
Not be able to lend glory to his subject,
But anyone who writes about you, if he can
simply tell
Who you are, will find his writing has dignity.
Let him copy down what is written in you,
And not make worse what nature has made so
clear,
And he will have created a copy that will make
him famous
And cause his style to be admired everywhere.
You add a curse to your beautiful blessings,
By being fond of praise, which only makes your
praises worse.

Sonnet LXXXV

My tongue-tied Muse in manners holds her still,
While comments of your praise, richly compiled,
Reserve their character with golden quill
And precious phrase by all the Muses filed.
I think good thoughts whilst other write good words,
And like unletter'd clerk still cry 'Amen'
To every hymn that able spirit affords
In polish'd form of well-refined pen.
Hearing you praised, I say "Tis so, 'tis true,'
And to the most of praise add something more;
But that is in my thought, whose love to you,
Though words come hindmost, holds his rank before.
Then others for the breath of words respect,
Me for my dumb thoughts, speaking in effect.

My Muse politely stays quiet
While comments praising you are created in abundance,
Retaining their distinctive style in golden words
And precious phrases made smoother by all the Muses.
I think good thoughts while others write good words,
And like an uneducated clerk still cry 'Amen!'
To every poem that stronger poets offer
In the polished form of a well-refined style.
Hearing you praised, I say 'It is so, it is true,'
And to even the most praise, I add something more,
But it is in my thoughts, where love for you,
Comes first before the words.
Respect others who praise you in breath and words,
And me for doing so in my silent thoughts, speaking what is true.

Sonnet LXXXVI

Was it the proud full sail of his great verse,
Bound for the prize of all too precious you,
That did my ripe thoughts in my brain inhearse,
Making their tomb the womb wherein they grew?
Was it his spirit, by spirits taught to write
Above a mortal pitch, that struck me dead?
No, neither he, nor his compeers by night
Giving him aid, my verse astonished.
He, nor that affable familiar ghost
Which nightly gulls him with intelligence
As victors of my silence cannot boast;
I was not sick of any fear from thence:
But when your countenance fill'd up his line,
Then lack'd I matter; that enfeebled mine.

Was it the way his poem sailed like a ship in full sail,
Headed for the prize of the all too precious you,
That buried the fully prepared thoughts in my head,
Making a grave of the womb where they grew?
Was it his energy, the way he was taught by dead poets
To write like no living man can, that struck me dead?
No, it wasn't him, or his associates that came in the night
To give him help that struck me dumb.
Neither he or that friendly and familiar ghost
That deceives him with false information
Can boast to have have silenced me;
I was not sickened by fear of them:
But when you looked favorably on his poems,
I suddenly lacked subject-matter and my poems became weak.

Sonnet LXXXVII

Farewell! thou art too dear for my possessing,
And like enough thou know'st thy estimate:
The charter of thy worth gives thee releasing;
My bonds in thee are all determinate.
For how do I hold thee but by thy granting?
And for that riches where is my deserving?
The cause of this fair gift in me is wanting,
And so my patent back again is swerving.
Thyself thou gavest, thy own worth then not knowing,
Or me, to whom thou gavest it, else mistaking;
So thy great gift, upon misprision growing,
Comes home again, on better judgment making.
Thus have I had thee, as a dream doth flatter,
In sleep a king, but waking no such matter.

Goodbye! You are too valuable for me to have,
And likely enough, you are aware of your worth.
The privilege of your worth gives you the right to let me go;
My ties to you have been terminated.
How could I hold onto unless you granted it?
And how could I even possibly deserve to do so?
I have nothing in me that shows I am entitled to this gift,
And you must have given me the right to it in error.
Perhaps when you gave it to me, you did not know its worth,
Or else you were mistaken about me when you gave it.
So the great gift, given based on an error you are now seeing,
Goes back to you, now that your judgment is better.
And so I had you, and it was like dreaming
In my sleep I was a king, only to wake to find this is not the case.

Sonnet LXXXVIII

When thou shalt be disposed to set me light,
And place my merit in the eye of scorn,
Upon thy side against myself I'll fight,
And prove thee virtuous, though thou art forsworn.
With mine own weakness being best acquainted,
Upon thy part I can set down a story
Of faults conceal'd, wherein I am attainted,
That thou in losing me shalt win much glory:
And I by this will be a gainer too;
For bending all my loving thoughts on thee,
The injuries that to myself I do,
Doing thee vantage, double-vantage me.
Such is my love, to thee I so belong,
That for thy right myself will bear all wrong.

When you feel inclined to place in me little value
And make my worthlessness an object of scorn,
I will take your side against myself,
And prove your virtue, even though you will be lying.
I am well acquainted with my weaknesses,
And, supporting your story, I can tell a story
About my hidden faults and say I am tainted,
And that you were right in leaving me:
By doing this I will find a gain,
Because by turning all of my loving thoughts toward you,
The harm that I do to myself,
Since it is to your advantage, is to my advantage, as well.
My love is so strong and I belong to you so completely
That I will carry everything that's wrong so that you may be right.

Sonnet LXXXIX

Say that thou didst forsake me for some fault,
And I will comment upon that offence;
Speak of my lameness, and I straight will halt,
Against thy reasons making no defence.
Thou canst not, love, disgrace me half so ill,
To set a form upon desired change,
As I'll myself disgrace: knowing thy will,
I will acquaintance strangle and look strange,
Be absent from thy walks, and in my tongue
Thy sweet beloved name no more shall dwell,
Lest I, too much profane, should do it wrong
And haply of our old acquaintance tell.
For thee against myself I'll vow debate,
For I must ne'er love him whom thou dost hate.

Say that you left me for some fault of mine,
And I will elaborate on whatever you say I did
wrong.
If you say I am lame, I will begin to limp
immediately,
And will not defend myself against your reasons.
You cannot, love, disgrace me half as badly,
As you find the reasons for having left me,
As I will disgrace myself, as soon as I know
what you need.
I will stop my acquaintance with you and act
like a stranger,
I won't be in the places where you walk, and on
my tongue
Your sweet, beloved name will no longer live,
Because I may say it in the wrong tone
And reveal how close we once were.
I vow to argue against myself for your sake,
Because I cannot love myself if that is whom you
hate.

Sonnet XC

Then hate me when thou wilt; if ever, now;
Now, while the world is bent my deeds to cross,
Join with the spite of fortune, make me bow,
And do not drop in for an after-loss:
Ah, do not, when my heart hath 'scoped this sorrow,
Come in the rearward of a conquer'd woe;
Give not a windy night a rainy morrow,
To linger out a purposed overthrow.
If thou wilt leave me, do not leave me last,
When other petty griefs have done their spite
But in the onset come; so shall I taste
At first the very worst of fortune's might,
And other strains of woe, which now seem woe,
Compared with loss of thee will not seem so.

So, hate me when you will; and if ever, now;
Now, while the world seems determined to mess up my life,
You should join in the streak of bad luck and cause me to collapse.
Don't drop it on me after all of my other losses are done:
Oh, do not do it when my heart has healed from this sorrow,
Do not come back again after I've gotten over my sadness.
Don't give a rainy tomorrow to my windy night,
Drawing out the sense of defeat I've had.
If you are going to leave me, don't wait to do it last,
When all of the other little sorrows have done their damage,
But do it no, so that I may taste
The worst of my bad fortune right away.
And all of the other sadness, which now seem so awful,
Will not seem so when compared to the loss of you.

Sonnet XCI

Some glory in their birth, some in their skill,
Some in their wealth, some in their bodies'
force,
Some in their garments, though new-fangled ill,
Some in their hawks and hounds, some in their
horse;
And every humour hath his adjunct pleasure,
Wherein it finds a joy above the rest:
But these particulars are not my measure;
All these I better in one general best.
Thy love is better than high birth to me,
Richer than wealth, prouder than garments' cost,
Of more delight than hawks or horses be;
And having thee, of all men's pride I boast:
Wretched in this alone, that thou mayst take
All this away and me most wretched make.

*Some people take pride in their birth, and some
in their skill,*
*Some in their wealth, and some in their physical
strength,*
*Some take pride in their clothes, though they are
badly new-fangled,*
*Some in their hawks and their hounds, some in
their horse;*
*And every personality has something extra it
takes pleasure in,*
That it finds joy in above everything else.
*But I do not measure my life by these sorts of
details,*
I have something that is better than all of this.
Your love is better than high birth to me,
*Richer than wealth, prouder than expensive
clothes,*
More delightful than hawks or horses could be,
And, having you, I boast the pride of all men:
*I'm only miserable in one regard—you might
take*
All of this away and leave me miserable.

Sonnet XCII

But do thy worst to steal thyself away,
For term of life thou art assured mine,
And life no longer than thy love will stay,
For it depends upon that love of thine.
Then need I not to fear the worst of wrongs,
When in the least of them my life hath end.
I see a better state to me belongs
Than that which on thy humour doth depend;
Thou canst not vex me with inconstant mind,
Since that my life on thy revolt doth lie.
O, what a happy title do I find,
Happy to have thy love, happy to die!
But what's so blessed-fair that fears no blot?
Thou mayst be false, and yet I know it not.

Go ahead and do the worst and leave me,
I live as long as you are mine,
And will not live any longer than you stay,
For my life depends upon your love.
So, I do not need to fear the worst of wrongs,
When, if you hurt me the least little bit, my life
will end.
I see now that I'm in a better position
Than if I depended on your feelings for me;
You can't trouble me with a fickle mind,
Since my life would end if you had a change of
heart.
Oh, what a happy situation I have found myself
in:
Happy to have your love, and happy to die!
But what position could be so blessed that I'd
have no worries?
You may be unfaithful to me, and I will not know
it.

Sonnet XCIII

So shall I live, supposing thou art true,
Like a deceived husband; so love's face
May still seem love to me, though alter'd new;
Thy looks with me, thy heart in other place:
For there can live no hatred in thine eye,
Therefore in that I cannot know thy change.
In many's looks the false heart's history
Is writ in moods and frowns and wrinkles
strange,
But heaven in thy creation did decree
That in thy face sweet love should ever dwell;
Whate'er thy thoughts or thy heart's workings
be,
Thy looks should nothing thence but sweetness
tell.
How like Eve's apple doth thy beauty grow,
if thy sweet virtue answer not thy show!

So I will live as if you are faithful,
In the same way a deceived husband does, so
that your face
Will still seem to hold love for me, even though
that has changed.
Your loving looks will be with me, but your
heart will be somewhere else:
And because no hatred could exist in your
expression,
I will never be able to see the change.
In the looks of many, the story of an unfaithful
heart
Is written in moodiness and frowns and strange
wrinkles,
But when heaven created you, you were given
A face on which only sweetness and love could
live.
Whatever you think or feel in your heart,
Your looks will express nothing but sweetness.
Your face is very much like Eve's apple, in that
way,
If you should ever stray from being sweet and
virtuous, it will not show!

Sonnet XCIV

They that have power to hurt and will do none,
That do not do the thing they most do show,
Who, moving others, are themselves as stone,
Unmoved, cold, and to temptation slow,
They rightly do inherit heaven's graces
And husband nature's riches from expense;
They are the lords and owners of their faces,
Others but stewards of their excellence.
The summer's flower is to the summer sweet,
Though to itself it only live and die,
But if that flower with base infection meet,
The basest weed outbraves his dignity:
For sweetest things turn sourest by their deeds;
Lilies that fester smell far worse than weeds.

Those that have the power to hurt others and do not,
That do not do the thing their looks say they could do,
Who, while moving others, are themselves like stone—
Unmoved, cold and slow to tempt—
They will rightfully inherit heaven's graces
And will keep nature's riches from being used up.
They are their own lord and own their appearance,
While everyone else is simply controlling their talents.
The summer's flower is sweet in the summer,
Though it sees itself only as living and dying,
But if that flower were infected with something wretched,
The lowest weed would have more dignity:
The sweetest things turn sourest by their actions;
Rotting lilies smell far worse than weeds.

Sonnet XCV

How sweet and lovely dost thou make the shame
Which, like a canker in the fragrant rose,
Doth spot the beauty of thy budding name!
O, in what sweets dost thou thy sins enclose!
That tongue that tells the story of thy days,
Making lascivious comments on thy sport,
Cannot dispraise but in a kind of praise;
Naming thy name blesses an ill report.
O, what a mansion have those vices got
Which for their habitation chose out thee,
Where beauty's veil doth cover every blot,
And all things turn to fair that eyes can see!
Take heed, dear heart, of this large privilege;
The hardest knife ill-used doth lose his edge.

You make shame look so sweet and lovely
While, like a canker in a fragrant rose,
It stains the beauty of your name!
Oh, you cover up your sins with such sweet
covers!
The tongue that tells yours story
And makes lustful comments about your sexual
recreation,
Cannot help but turn criticism into a kind of
praise;
Mentioning your name makes a bad thing look
good.
Oh, what a grand place those vices of yours
Get to live in, having chosen you,
Where your beauty covers every fault,
And turns everything that eyes can see to good!
Be careful, dear heart, of this great privilege:
The hardest knife, when used badly, will lose its
edge.

Sonnet XCVI

Some say thy fault is youth, some wantonness;
Some say thy grace is youth and gentle sport;
Both grace and faults are loved of more and less;
Thou makest faults graces that to thee resort.
As on the finger of a throned queen
The basest jewel will be well esteem'd,
So are those errors that in thee are seen
To truths translated and for true things deem'd.
How many lambs might the stern wolf betray,
If like a lamb he could his looks translate!
How many gazers mightst thou lead away,
If thou wouldst use the strength of all thy state!
But do not so; I love thee in such sort
As, thou being mine, mine is thy good report.

*Some say your fault is your youth, while others
say it is your promiscuity;
Some say your virtue is in your youth and
playfulness,
And your faults and virtues are more or less
loved by all;
You are capable of turning your faults into
virtues.
In the same way the finger of a queen on a
throne
Will make the lowest jewel seem vaulable,
So are the errors in you seen
As good things and regarded as good.
How many lambs might the prowling wolf
betray,
If he could make himself look like a lamb!
How many viewers you could lead away,
If you would use the power at your disposal!
But don't do that; I love you in such a way
That, since you are mine, your reputation
reflects on me.*

Sonnet XCVII

How like a winter hath my absence been
From thee, the pleasure of the fleeting year!
What freezings have I felt, what dark days seen!
What old December's bareness every where!
And yet this time removed was summer's time,
The teeming autumn, big with rich increase,
Bearing the wanton burden of the prime,
Like widow'd wombs after their lords' decease:
Yet this abundant issue seem'd to me
But hope of orphans and unfather'd fruit;
For summer and his pleasures wait on thee,
And, thou away, the very birds are mute;
Or, if they sing, 'tis with so dull a cheer
That leaves look pale, dreading the winter's
near.

It has felt like winter since I've been away
From you, since you give pleasure to the
passing year!
I have felt so cold and have seen such dark
days!
Old December's bareness was everywhere!
Despite the fact that our time apart was during
the summer,
And then into the overfull autumn, big with
abundance,
With harvest-time bearing the fruits of its prime,
Like a widow bears a child after her lord dies.
These abundant crops seemed to me
Like orphans and unfathered fruit;
The pleasure of summer depends on you,
And, when you are away, the birds are quiet,
Or, if they sing, they do it so dully,
That the leaves tune pale, dreading winter's
approach.

Sonnet XCVIII

From you have I been absent in the spring,
When proud-pied April dress'd in all his trim
Hath put a spirit of youth in every thing,
That heavy Saturn laugh'd and leap'd with him.
Yet nor the lays of birds nor the sweet smell
Of different flowers in odour and in hue
Could make me any summer's story tell,
Or from their proud lap pluck them where they grew;
Nor did I wonder at the lily's white,
Nor praise the deep vermilion in the rose;
They were but sweet, but figures of delight,
Drawn after you, you pattern of all those.
Yet seem'd it winter still, and, you away,
As with your shadow I with these did play.

I have been absent from you throughout the spring,
When splendid and colorful April dressed in all his finery
Put the spirit of youth into everything so much,
That even heavy old Saturn laughed and leaped with him.
Still, neither the songs of the birds nor the sweet scent
Of the different odors of colored flowers
Could make me feel like it was summer,
Or inspire me to pick them from where they grew.
I did not wonder at the white of the lily,
Or praise the deep red in the rose;
They were simply sweet figures of delight
That looked as if they have been drawn to your pattern.
It seemed like it was still winter with you away,
And I played with the flowers as if they were your ghost.

Sonnet XCIX

The forward violet thus did I chide:
Sweet thief, whence didst thou steal thy sweet that smells,
If not from my love's breath? The purple pride
Which on thy soft cheek for complexion dwells
In my love's veins thou hast too grossly dyed.
The lily I condemned for thy hand,
And buds of marjoram had stol'n thy hair:
The roses fearfully on thorns did stand,
One blushing shame, another white despair;
A third, nor red nor white, had stol'n of both
And to his robbery had annex'd thy breath;
But, for his theft, in pride of all his growth
A vengeful canker eat him up to death.
More flowers I noted, yet I none could see
But sweet or colour it had stol'n from thee.

I scolded the precocious violet:
'Sweet thief, where did you steal that scent that smells
Exactly like my love's breath? The purple color
Which is on your soft cheek for color lives
In my love's veins, and you have grossly dyed
yourself in it.'
I condemned the lily for stealing the whiteness
of your hand,
And the buds of marjoram for stealing your hair.
The roses trembled in fear, standing on their thorns,
With one blushing red in shame and another white in despair;
A third, neither red nor white, had stolen both colors,
And to his robbery added your breath.
And, because of his theft, when he was in the pride of his growth
A terrible parasite ate him to death.
I saw more flowers, and there were none I could see
That hadn't stolen their scent or color from you.

Sonnet C

Where art thou, Muse, that thou forget'st so long
To speak of that which gives thee all thy might?
Spend'st thou thy fury on some worthless song,
Darkening thy power to lend base subjects light?
Return, forgetful Muse, and straight redeem
In gentle numbers time so idly spent;
Sing to the ear that doth thy lays esteem
And gives thy pen both skill and argument.
Rise, resty Muse, my love's sweet face survey,
If Time have any wrinkle graven there;
If any, be a satire to decay,
And make Time's spoils despised every where.
Give my love fame faster than Time wastes life;
So thou prevent'st his scythe and crooked knife.

Where are you, Muse, that you have forgotten
for so long
To speak of the subject that gives you all your
strength?
Have you been spending your fierce passion on
some worthless song,
And depriving your power by lending low
subjects light?
Come back, forgetful Muse, and redeem yourself
And make up for your idle time by inspiring
some gentle poems;
Sing into the ear that values you
And which provides your pen with both skill and
a subject.
Rise, lazy Muse, and look at my love's sweet
face,
If Time has carved any wrinkles there,
Compose a satire to decay,
And make Time's ruins despised everywhere.
Give my love fame faster than Time can waste
life;
And in that way you can prevent his scythe and
crooked knife.

Sonnet CI

O truant Muse, what shall be thy amends
For thy neglect of truth in beauty dyed?
Both truth and beauty on my love depends;
So dost thou too, and therein dignified.
Make answer, Muse: wilt thou not haply say
'Truth needs no colour, with his colour fix'd;
Beauty no pencil, beauty's truth to lay;
But best is best, if never intermix'd?'
Because he needs no praise, wilt thou be dumb?
Excuse not silence so; for't lies in thee
To make him much outlive a gilded tomb,
And to be praised of ages yet to be.
Then do thy office, Muse; I teach thee how
To make him seem long hence as he shows now.

So, truant Muse, how are you going to make amends
For neglecting truth that is colored in beauty?
Both truth and beauty depend on my love,
And you do, too, and are dignified in that way.
Answer me, Muse: perhaps you will say
'Truth needs no color, since his color is already fixed to beauty;
And beauty needs no fine-pointed paintbrush; beauty is layered in truth;
Is whatever is best the best when not mixed with anything?'
Because he requires no praise, will you be silent?
There is no excuse for the silence, since it lies within you
To make him live beyond a golden tomb,
And to be praised for ages to come.
So, do your job, Muse; I will teach you how
To make him appear as he appears now in the future.

Sonnet CII

My love is strengthen'd, though more weak in
seeming;
I love not less, though less the show appear:
That love is merchandized whose rich esteeming
The owner's tongue doth publish every where.
Our love was new and then but in the spring
When I was wont to greet it with my lays,
As Philomel in summer's front doth sing
And stops her pipe in growth of riper days:
Not that the summer is less pleasant now
Than when her mournful hymns did hush the
night,
But that wild music burthens every bough
And sweets grown common lose their dear
delight.
Therefore like her I sometime hold my tongue,
Because I would not dull you with my song.

*My love is stronger, although is seems to be
weaker;*
I don't love you less; I just show it less often.
*Love is turned into merchandise by the high
praise*
That the owner announces everywhere.
Our love was new and in its spring
When I was inclined to greet it with poems
*In the way Philomela sings songs at the
beginning of summer*
*Then stops singing so much as the days grow
ripe;*
It's not because summer is less pleasant then
*Than when she sang her mournful tunes in the
quiet of night,*
*But that wild music and songs now burden every
bough*
*And sweets that have grown common lose their
delight.*
So, like her, I sometimes hold my tongue,
Because I do not want to bore you with my song.

Sonnet CIII

Alack, what poverty my Muse brings forth,
That having such a scope to show her pride,
The argument all bare is of more worth
Than when it hath my added praise beside!
O, blame me not, if I no more can write!
Look in your glass, and there appears a face
That over-goes my blunt invention quite,
Dulling my lines and doing me disgrace.
Were it not sinful then, striving to mend,
To mar the subject that before was well?
For to no other pass my verses tend
Than of your graces and your gifts to tell;
And more, much more, than in my verse can sit
Your own glass shows you when you look in it.

Alas, my Muse brings forth only poverty,
Since even with a big subject to show off her skill,
The subject, which is you, is worth more
Than when I have not added my praise to it!
Oh, don't blame me, if I can't write anymore!
Look in your mirror, and there you will see a face
That exceeds my blunt and limited inventions,
Making my lines dull and causing me disgrace.
Wouldn't it be a sin if—while trying to improve—
I messed up a subject that was already quite well?
I write about nothing else in my poems except you,
Describing your graces and your gifts;
And more, much more, than my poems can contain
Your own mirror shows when you look into it.

Sonnet CIV

To me, fair friend, you never can be old,
For as you were when first your eye I eyed,
Such seems your beauty still. Three winters cold
Have from the forests shook three summers'
pride,
Three beauteous springs to yellow autumn turn'd
In process of the seasons have I seen,
Three April perfumes in three hot Junes burn'd,
Since first I saw you fresh, which yet are green.
Ah! yet doth beauty, like a dial-hand,
Steal from his figure and no pace perceived;
So your sweet hue, which methinks still doth
stand,
Hath motion and mine eye may be deceived:
For fear of which, hear this, thou age unbred;
Ere you were born was beauty's summer dead.

You'll never be old to me, fair friend—
The way you looked when I first eyed your eye—
That is how you still look. Three cold winters
Have shook three summers' worth of leaves
from the forests,
And three beautiful springs have turned to
autumn's yellow
In the passing of the seasons I have seen;
Three perfumed Aprils have burned into three
hot Junes,
Since I first saw you fresh, and you're still green
and new.
Oh! Still, beauty, like a clock's hand,
Steals from his figure with a pace so slow it is
not perceived;
So your sweet complexion, which seems to me to
stand still,
Has motion, and my eye may be deceived.
For fear that it is, hear this, future generations
not yet conceived:
Before you were born, the greatest beauty was
already dead.

Sonnet CV

Let not my love be call'd idolatry,
Nor my beloved as an idol show,
Since all alike my songs and praises be
To one, of one, still such, and ever so.
Kind is my love to-day, to-morrow kind,
Still constant in a wondrous excellence;
Therefore my verse to constancy confined,
One thing expressing, leaves out difference.
'Fair, kind and true' is all my argument,
'Fair, kind, and true' varying to other words;
And in this change is my invention spent,
Three themes in one, which wondrous scope
affords.
'Fair, kind, and true,' have often lived alone,
Which three till now never kept seat in one.

Let no one call my love idolatry,
Or say that my beloved is an idol show,
Since my songs and praises are all alike
And are to one, of one, have been, and will
always be.
My love is kind today, and kind tomorrow.
And is constant in an extraordinary excellence;
So my poems are confined to that constancy,
Expressing one thing, and leaving out anything
different.
'Fair, kind, and true' is the entire subject of my
poems.
'Fair, kind, and true' is what I write about in
various ways,
And it is in this variation that I spend my
creativity.
These three themes are contained in one,
providing a broad subject.
'Fair, kind, and true' are traits often found
alone,
But the three traits were never all in one person
until now.

Sonnet CVI

When in the chronicle of wasted time
I see descriptions of the fairest wights,
And beauty making beautiful old rhyme
In praise of ladies dead and lovely knights,
Then, in the blazon of sweet beauty's best,
Of hand, of foot, of lip, of eye, of brow,
I see their antique pen would have express'd
Even such a beauty as you master now.
So all their praises are but prophecies
Of this our time, all you prefiguring;
And, for they look'd but with divining eyes,
They had not skill enough your worth to sing:
For we, which now behold these present days,
Had eyes to wonder, but lack tongues to praise.

When I read accounts about times past
And I see descriptions of the most favorable
people,
And read beautiful poems inspired by their
beauty,
That praise the ladies who are dead and the
lovely knights,
When I read the accounts of their best
features—
Their hands, their feet, their lips, their eyes,
their foreheads—
I see how their antique poet would have
expressed
Even such a beauty as you have now.
All of their praises where just prophecies
Of our time, and they prefigure you;
And, even though they see with foretelling eyes,
They did not have enough skill to sing your
worth:
Just like we, who now look at these present
days,
Have the eyes to wonder, but lack the words to
praise.

Sonnet CVII

Not mine own fears, nor the prophetic soul
Of the wide world dreaming on things to come,
Can yet the lease of my true love control,
Supposed as forfeit to a confined doom.
The mortal moon hath her eclipse endured
And the sad augurs mock their own presage;
Incertainties now crown themselves assured
And peace proclaims olives of endless age.
Now with the drops of this most balmy time
My love looks fresh, and death to me subscribes,
Since, spite of him, I'll live in this poor rhyme,
While he insults o'er dull and speechless tribes:
And thou in this shalt find thy monument,
When tyrants' crests and tombs of brass are spent.

Neither my own fears or the collective predictions
Of the wide world dreaming about things to come,
Can keep me from owning my true love,
Who was supposed to have remained confined.
The mortal moon has endured her eclipse
And the sad fortune tellers ridicule their own forecasts;
Things that were uncertain can now be crowned as certain,
And peace proclaims itself to stay for an endless amount of time.
Now, sprinkled with the drops of this healing time,
My love looks fresh again, and death yields to me,
Since, in spite of death, I'll live on in this poor poem,
While he triumphs over ignorant and speechless people:
And you will find in this poem your monument,
When tyrants' crests and tombs of brass have wasted away.

Sonnet CVIII

What's in the brain that ink may character
Which hath not figured to thee my true spirit?
What's new to speak, what new to register,
That may express my love or thy dear merit?
Nothing, sweet boy; but yet, like prayers divine,
I must, each day say o'er the very same,
Counting no old thing old, thou mine, I thine,
Even as when first I hallow'd thy fair name.
So that eternal love in love's fresh case
Weighs not the dust and injury of age,
Nor gives to necessary wrinkles place,
But makes antiquity for aye his page,
Finding the first conceit of love there bred
Where time and outward form would show it
dead.

What's in the brain that ink may form into
characters,
Which I haven't written to show you of my
faithful spirit?
What's new to say, what's new to record
That may express my love or your great merit?
Nothing, sweet boy, and still, like divine
prayers,
I must say the same thing over and over,
Counting nothing old as old; you are mine, and
I am yours
In the same way as when I first honored your
fair name.
Eternal love dressed in fresh love's suit
Does not take into consideration the dust and
injury of age,
Nor does it acknowledge your wrinkles,
But makes old age forever his servant,
Finding the original inspiration for love where
it was born,
Even though time and outward appearance
would make it appear to be dead.

Sonnet CIX

O, never say that I was false of heart,
Though absence seem'd my flame to qualify.
As easy might I from myself depart
As from my soul, which in thy breast doth lie:
That is my home of love: if I have ranged,
Like him that travels I return again,
Just to the time, not with the time exchanged,
So that myself bring water for my stain.
Never believe, though in my nature reign'd
All frailties that besiege all kinds of blood,
That it could so preposterously be stain'd,
To leave for nothing all thy sum of good;
For nothing this wide universe I call,
Save thou, my rose; in it thou art my all.

Oh, never say that I was unfaithful to you in my heart,
Even though absence made it seem my flame had weakened.
I may as easily depart myself from myself
As from my soul, which lies inside my breast:
Your love is my home, and if I had wandered,
Like one who travels, I would return again,
Exactly on time, with nothing changed,
Bringing my own water to cleanse my disgrace.
Don't ever believe, just because in my nature I have
The weaknesses that trouble all kinds of blood,
That my nature could be so ridiculously dishonored,
That I would leave all of your good for nothing;
There is nothing in the entire universe I visit
Except for you, my rose. You are everything to me.

Sonnet CX

Alas, 'tis true I have gone here and there
And made myself a motley to the view,
Gored mine own thoughts, sold cheap what is most dear,
Made old offences of affections new;
Most true it is that I have look'd on truth
Askance and strangely: but, by all above,
These blenches gave my heart another youth,
And worse essays proved thee my best of love.
Now all is done, have what shall have no end:
Mine appetite I never more will grind
On newer proof, to try an older friend,
A god in love, to whom I am confined.
Then give me welcome, next my heaven the best,
Even to thy pure and most most loving breast.

Alas, it is true that I have gone here and there,
And made myself look like a fool,
I've wounded my own thoughts, made cheap what is of value,
And have committed old wrongs with my new friends;
It's entirely true that I've looked at truth
Scornfully, as if it were strange, but, I swear by heaven,
Theses turns made my heart young again,
And the worst tests have proved that I love you best.
Now I'm done with all of that, and I want what will have no end:
I will never again sharpen my appetite,
On new proof to test my feelings for an old friend,
The god of love to whom I am bound.
So give me welcome, you are the next best thing to heaven,
Allow me into your pure and most loving heart.

Sonnet CXI

O, for my sake do you with Fortune chide,
The guilty goddess of my harmful deeds,
That did not better for my life provide
Than public means which public manners
breeds.
Thence comes it that my name receives a brand,
And almost thence my nature is subdued
To what it works in, like the dyer's hand:
Pity me then and wish I were renew'd;
Whilst, like a willing patient, I will drink
Potions of eisel 'gainst my strong infection
No bitterness that I will bitter think,
Nor double penance, to correct correction.
Pity me then, dear friend, and I assure ye
Even that your pity is enough to cure me.

Oh, I know you curse my bad luck for my sake—
The guilty goddess of my hurtful deeds—
For not having a better way to make a living
Than by being in front of the public, which bred
public manners.
So it is that my name has received a bad mark,
And it has brought down my very nature,
To what it works in, like the dyer's hand covered
with ink:
So, take pity on me and hope that I can be
renewed,
While I, like a willing patient, will drink
Potions made with vinegar to clear up my
infection,
And I will not think any bitterness is bitter,
Not will I protest a double penance to try to
correct things.
Pity me, dear friend, and I assure you
That even your pity is enough to cure me.

Sonnet CXII

Your love and pity doth the impression fill
Which vulgar scandal stamp'd upon my brow;
For what care I who calls me well or ill,
So you o'er-green my bad, my good allow?
You are my all the world, and I must strive
To know my shames and praises from your
tongue:
None else to me, nor I to none alive,
That my steel'd sense or changes right or wrong.
In so profound abysm I throw all care
Of others' voices, that my adder's sense
To critic and to flatterer stopped are.
Mark how with my neglect I do dispense:
You are so strongly in my purpose bred
That all the world besides methinks are dead.

Your love and pity fill in the indentation
That vulgar scandal has stamped onto my
forehead.
What do I care who calls me good or bad,
As long as you gloss over my bad, and allow for
my good?
You are my entire world, and I must strive
To learn about my shames and praises from
you:
No one else matters to me, and I matter to no
one alive,
You can change my hardened sense whether it is
right or wrong.
Into a deep chasm I throw all care
Regarding the opinions of others, and my snake-
like awareness
Of criticism and flattery no longer works.
Notice how I disregard the neglect I am shown:
You are so strongly the main purpose of my life,
That it seems to me that the rest of the world is
dead.

Sonnet CXIII

Since I left you, mine eye is in my mind;
And that which governs me to go about
Doth part his function and is partly blind,
Seems seeing, but effectually is out;
For it no form delivers to the heart
Of bird of flower, or shape, which it doth latch:
Of his quick objects hath the mind no part,
Nor his own vision holds what it doth catch:
For if it see the rudest or gentlest sight,
The most sweet favour or deformed'st creature,
The mountain or the sea, the day or night,
The crow or dove, it shapes them to your
feature:
Incapable of more, replete with you,
My most true mind thus makes mine eye untrue.

Since I left you, my vision is turned inward,
And the part of me that controls my movement
Is half working and is half blind;
It sees things but it doesn't register them,
And it doesn't recognize the forms it sends to my
heart,
Such as birds or flowers or any shape it latches
onto;
The mind plays no part in recognizing these
objects,
And does not see what vision catches sight of,
Whether it's the crudest or gentlest sight,
The sweetest appearing or the most deformed
creature,
The mountain or the sea, the day or night,
The crow or dove—it makes them all look like
you.
Incapable of seeing anything else and full of
you,
My mind is faithful but is causing me to see
everything wrong.

Sonnet CXIV

Or whether doth my mind, being crown'd with you,
Drink up the monarch's plague, this flattery?
Or whether shall I say, mine eye saith true,
And that your love taught it this alchemy,
To make of monsters and things indigest
Such cherubins as your sweet self resemble,
Creating every bad a perfect best,
As fast as objects to his beams assemble?
O,'tis the first; 'tis flattery in my seeing,
And my great mind most kingly drinks it up:
Mine eye well knows what with his gust is 'greeing,
And to his palate doth prepare the cup:
If it be poison'd, 'tis the lesser sin
That mine eye loves it and doth first begin.

Does my mind, being invested with you,
Drink in the kingly affliction of flattery and delusion?
Or is it that what my eye sees is real,
And that your love has magically taught it how to alter things?
It has the ability to make monsters and deformed creatures
Into angels that sweetly resemble you,
And of creating every bad thing into a perfect best,
As soon as it comes into my line of vision.
Oh, it must be the first: my vision is full of delusions,
And my mind drinks it up like a king wanting flattery.
My eye knows well what my mind wants to see,
And prepares a cup the mind will relish:
If the cup is poisoned with falsehood, there is no harm,
My eye loves the false visions, too, and tastes them first.

Sonnet CXV

Those lines that I before have writ do lie,
Even those that said I could not love you dearer:
Yet then my judgment knew no reason why
My most full flame should afterwards burn clearer.
But reckoning time, whose million'd accidents
Creep in 'twixt vows and change decrees of kings,
Tan sacred beauty, blunt the sharp'st intents,
Divert strong minds to the course of altering things;
Alas, why, fearing of time's tyranny,
Might I not then say 'Now I love you best,'
When I was certain o'er incertainty,
Crowning the present, doubting of the rest?
Love is a babe; then might I not say so,
To give full growth to that which still doth grow?

Those lines I wrote before tell lies,
Even those that said I could not love you more:
Then my judgment knew of no reason why
My fullest flame for you could ever burn clearer.
But time has passed, with a million accidents
Having crept in between our values that are
capable of changing the decrees of kings,
Darkening sacred beauty, making the sharpest
intentions dull,
And forcing strong minds to adjust to a
changing course;
Alas, why then, fearful of time's tyranny,
Did I not say then, 'Now I love you best,'
When I was more certain than uncertain,
And I believed the present was complete, despite
doubts about the future?
Love is a baby, so couldn't I say
That even full grown, it will still continue to
grow?

Sonnet CXVI

Let me not to the marriage of true minds
Admit impediments. Love is not love
Which alters when it alteration finds,
Or bends with the remover to remove:
O no! it is an ever-fixed mark
That looks on tempests and is never shaken;
It is the star to every wandering bark,
Whose worth's unknown, although his height be taken.
Love's not Time's fool, though rosy lips and cheeks
Within his bending sickle's compass come:
Love alters not with his brief hours and weeks,
But bears it out even to the edge of doom.
If this be error and upon me proved,
I never writ, nor no man ever loved.

When it comes to the marriage of true minds,
I hope I will never admit there are obstacles.
Love is not love
If it changes when it sees change in the loved one,
Or if it turns in a new direction when the lover leaves:
Oh, no! It is a constant and fixed mark
That looks upon storms and is not shaken;
It is like the star that guides the way of every wandering ship,
And whose worth is unknown, although its actual height can be measured.
Love is not Time's fool, even though rosy lips and cheeks
Come within the compass of Time's altering sickle:
Love does not change with the passing of brief hours and weeks,
But will last even past the end of time.
If I am wrong and you can prove it,
Then I never wrote, and no man ever loved.

Sonnet CXVII

Accuse me thus: that I have scanted all
Wherein I should your great deserts repay,
Forgot upon your dearest love to call,
Whereto all bonds do tie me day by day;
That I have frequent been with unknown minds
And given to time your own dear-purchased
right
That I have hoisted sail to all the winds
Which should transport me farthest from your
sight.
Book both my wilfulness and errors down
And on just proof surmise accumulate;
Bring me within the level of your frown,
But shoot not at me in your waken'd hate;
Since my appeal says I did strive to prove
The constancy and virtue of your love.

Accuse me in this way: say that I have withheld
When I should have been repaying what was
greatly due to you,
And I forgot to call upon your dearest love,
Even though I am bound to you every day;
Say that I've spent too much time with people
you don't know
And have given away the time you have
purchased by right,
And that I have hoisted my sail and rode all the
winds
That could transport me the farthest away from
your sight.
Write and list my stubborn ways and all the
errors I've committed,
And guess about all the things I've done you
have no proof of.
Bring me to the level of your frown
But don't shoot at me because I've awakened
your hatred;
I only did it in an effort to test
The constancy and honesty of your love for me.

Sonnet CXVIII

Like as, to make our appetites more keen,
With eager compounds we our palate urge,
As, to prevent our maladies unseen,
We sicken to shun sickness when we purge,
Even so, being tuff of your ne'er-cloying
sweetness,
To bitter sauces did I frame my feeding
And, sick of welfare, found a kind of meetness
To be diseased ere that there was true needing.
Thus policy in love, to anticipate
The ills that were not, grew to faults assured
And brought to medicine a healthful state
Which, rank of goodness, would by ill be cured:
But thence I learn, and find the lesson true,
Drugs poison him that so fell sick of you.

*In the same way that we make our appetites
sharper,
By eating bitter combinations of food,
And, in order to prevent unknown illnesses,
We force ourselves to vomit and purge,
In the same way, being full of your sweetness,
I turned to feed on bitter sauces.
Tired of feeling well, I found myself ready
To make myself sick before I needed to be sick.
With this policy in place, I anticipated
Problems that didn't exist and faults that were
not there,
And brought medicine to a healthy state of
being,
Which was abundant in goodness, and I tried to
cure it with bad:
But what I learned from doing this—and I find
this lesson to be true—
Is that the drugs poisoned me because I am so
lovesick over you.*

Sonnet CXIX

What potions have I drunk of Siren tears,
Distill'd from limbecks foul as hell within,
Applying fears to hopes and hopes to fears,
Still losing when I saw myself to win!
What wretched errors hath my heart committed,
Whilst it hath thought itself so blessed never!
How have mine eyes out of their spheres been fitted
In the distraction of this madding fever!
O benefit of ill! now I find true
That better is by evil still made better;
And ruin'd love, when it is built anew,
Grows fairer than at first, more strong, far greater.
So I return rebuked to my content
And gain by ill thrice more than I have spent.

I've drank potions that seemed sweet, like a Siren's tears,
Which were distilled and foul as hell inside;
I've applied fears to hopes and hopes to fears,
Always losing when I imagined I would win!
My heart has made so many awful mistakes,
While it was thinking it had never been so blessed!
My eyes have rolled out of their sockets
Due to the distraction of this maddening fever!
Oh, the benefits of illness! Now I see it's true
That good is made better by evil;
Ruined love, when it is made new again,
Grows more beautiful than it originally was,
and stronger and far greater.
And so I return after being shamed by the one who makes me happy,
And find I have gained by my bad actions three times more than I spent.

Sonnet CXX

That you were once unkind befriends me now,
And for that sorrow which I then did feel
Needs must I under my transgression bow,
Unless my nerves were brass or hammer'd steel.
For if you were by my unkindness shaken
As I by yours, you've pass'd a hell of time,
And I, a tyrant, have no leisure taken
To weigh how once I suffered in your crime.
O, that our night of woe might have remember'd
My deepest sense, how hard true sorrow hits,
And soon to you, as you to me, then tender'd
The humble slave which wounded bosoms fits!
But that your trespass now becomes a fee;
Mine ransoms yours, and yours must ransom me.

The fact that you were once unkind to me is helpful to me now,
And because of the sorrow I felt then,
I have to bow down out of shame for the wrong I've done,
Otherwise my nerves would be made of brass or steel.
Because if you were shaken by my unkindness In the same way as I have been by yours, then you had a hell of a time,
And I, like a tyrant, have not taken the time To consider how I once suffered the same way due to your crime against me.
Oh, how I wish I had remembered our earlier night of sadness,
So that I would have sensed how hard sorrow can hit,
And I would have apologized sooner, as you had to me,
Since it is the humble slave that best attends to wounded hearts.
So, your earlier wrong against me becomes a fee,
And mine cancels out yours, as yours cancels out mine.

Sonnet CXXI

'Tis better to be vile than vile esteem'd,
When not to be receives reproach of being,
And the just pleasure lost which is so deem'd
Not by our feeling but by others' seeing:
For why should others false adulterate eyes
Give salutation to my sportive blood?
Or on my frailties why are frailer spies,
Which in their wills count bad what I think good?
No, I am that I am, and they that level
At my abuses reckon up their own:
I may be straight, though they themselves be bevel;
By their rank thoughts my deeds must not be shown;
Unless this general evil they maintain,
All men are bad, and in their badness reign.

It's better to be vile than thought to be vile,
Since if you are not you get the blame for being so,
And you don't even get to experience the pleasure
Of being the thing that others think is so vile:
Why should others who have false and adulterous eyes
Get to address my amorous blood so knowingly?
And why should people weaker than me get to spy on my weaknesses,
And get to say that what I think is good is bad?
No, I am what I am, and they that charge
Me for my wrongs are counting up their own:
It may be that I am straight while they are crooked;
You can't gauge my actions by their thoughts;
Unless they are willing to defend
That all men are bad and have power in their badness.

Sonnet CXXII

Thy gift, thy tables, are within my brain
Full character'd with lasting memory,
Which shall above that idle rank remain
Beyond all date, even to eternity;
Or at the least, so long as brain and heart
Have faculty by nature to subsist;
Till each to razed oblivion yield his part
Of thee, thy record never can be miss'd.
That poor retention could not so much hold,
Nor need I tallies thy dear love to score;
Therefore to give them from me was I bold,
To trust those tables that receive thee more:
To keep an adjunct to remember thee
Were to import forgetfulness in me.

*The gift you gave me—the notebooks—are
already full in my mind*
Written in characters that stay in my memory,
*Which will remain longer than the books
themselves,*
Beyond all dates and into eternity.
*Or, at the very least, as long as my brain and
heart*
Have their full power and live on;
*Until each is erased into forgetfulness and gives
up part*
Of you, the record cannot be missed.
*The humble method of retaining information
could not hold much,*
*And I don't need to keep notes to keep my
account of you, anyway,*
So I was bold enough to give them away,
*Trusting my own memory to remember more
about you:*
To use an aid to help remember you,
Would seem to suggest I am forgetful.

Sonnet CXXIII

No, Time, thou shalt not boast that I do change:
Thy pyramids built up with newer might
To me are nothing novel, nothing strange;
They are but dressings of a former sight.
Our dates are brief, and therefore we admire
What thou dost foist upon us that is old,
And rather make them born to our desire
Than think that we before have heard them told.
Thy registers and thee I both defy,
Not wondering at the present nor the past,
For thy records and what we see doth lie,
Made more or less by thy continual haste.
This I do vow and this shall ever be;
I will be true, despite thy scythe and thee.

No, Time, I will not allow you to boast that I change:
The pillars built up to be stronger and higher
Are nothing new or strange to me;
They are simply new versions of an old sight.
Our lives are brief, and so we admire
When you pass off old things on us
And make us think they are newly made just for us
Instead of admitting we have heard of them before.
I defy both you and your records,
I do not wonder about the present or the past,
Because both your records and what we see lie
As they are raised up and destroyed in constant haste.
I vow that this will always be the case:
I will be faithful, despite you and what you are capable of doing.

Sonnet CXXIV

If my dear love were but the child of state,
It might for Fortune's bastard be unfather'd'
As subject to Time's love or to Time's hate,
Weeds among weeds, or flowers with flowers gather'd.
No, it was builded far from accident;
It suffers not in smiling pomp, nor falls
Under the blow of thralled discontent,
Whereto the inviting time our fashion calls:
It fears not policy, that heretic,
Which works on leases of short-number'd hours,
But all alone stands hugely politic,
That it nor grows with heat nor drowns with showers.
To this I witness call the fools of time,
Which die for goodness, who have lived for crime.

If my love for you were simply the child of circumstance,
It might be claimed to be illegitimate
Since it would be subject to the favor or destruction of Time,
And could end up either as a weed among weeds, or a flower picked from flowers.
But my love for you was made in a place where accidents don't happen;
It does not have to be approved by nobility, or worry about falling
Under the blows of the enslaved and discontent,
Although the conventions of our times could invite either.
It does not have to fear shifts in policy brought about by disagreement,
Which only come about for short periods of time.
It stands alone, crafty and discrete,
And neither grows during heat nor drowns from showers.
I will call on the fools of time to be my witness, those
Who died good after living lives of crime.

Sonnet CXXV

Were 't aught to me I bore the canopy,
With my extern the outward honouring,
Or laid great bases for eternity,
Which prove more short than waste or ruining?
Have I not seen dwellers on form and favour
Lose all, and more, by paying too much rent,
For compound sweet forgoing simple savour,
Pitiful thrivers, in their gazing spent?
No, let me be obsequious in thy heart,
And take thou my oblation, poor but free,
Which is not mix'd with seconds, knows no art,
But mutual render, only me for thee.
Hence, thou suborn'd informer! a true soul
When most impeach'd stands least in thy control.

Would it be anything to me if I carried the veil in a royal procession,
Honored outwardly in appearance by doing so?
Of if I laid important foundations that are supposed to last for eternity,
But which will only last until they are ravaged and ruined?
Haven't I seen those who focus on appearance and favor
Lose everything, and more, by paying too much for them?
They forgo simple scents in an attempt to gain combined scents—
Tender wannabes who spend so much time in an expectant stance.
No, let me be dutiful to your heart,
And please take my gift, which is humble but freely given,
And not of inferior quality, and knows of nothing
But mutual surrender—me to you.
So, go away, you paid informer! A faithful soul
Like me is not in your control when accused.

Sonnet CXXVI

O thou, my lovely boy, who in thy power
Dost hold Time's fickle glass, his sickle, hour;
Who hast by waning grown, and therein show'st
Thy lovers withering as thy sweet self grow'st;
If Nature, sovereign mistress over wrack,
As thou goest onwards, still will pluck thee
back,
She keeps thee to this purpose, that her skill
May time disgrace and wretched minutes kill.
Yet fear her, O thou minion of her pleasure!
She may detain, but not still keep, her treasure:
Her audit, though delay'd, answer'd must be,
And her quietus is to render thee.

Oh you, my lovely boy, who holds in your power
Time's fickle mirror, his sickle and the hour;
Who has diminished in size, and in doing so,
Reveal how much I've withered while you
continue to grow sweet;
If Nature, the royal mistress over ruin,
Keeps you from aging as you move forward,
She does so to show off her skill,
Which time will disgrace as its wretched
minutes kill.
Still, you should fear her, oh you favorite of her
pleasures!
She may hold you back, but will not keep you as
her treasure:
Her accounting, although delayed, needs to be
answered,
And she will discharge of her debts with you.

Sonnet CXXVII

In the old age was not counted fair,
Or if it were, it bore not beauty's name;
But now is black beauty's successive heir,
And beauty slander'd with a bastard shame:
For since each hand hath put on nature's power,
Fairing the foul with art's false borrow'd face,
Sweet beauty hath no name, no holy bower,
But is profaned, if not lives in disgrace.
Therefore my mistress' brows are raven black,
Her eyes so suited, and they mourners seem
At such who, not born fair, no beauty lack,
Slandering creation with a false esteem:
Yet so they mourn, becoming of their woe,
That every tongue says beauty should look so.

In the old days, dark complexions were not considered beautiful,
Or, if they were, no one gave them beauty's name;
But these days, dark is considered rightfully beautiful,
And beauty is slandered with an illegitimate shame:
Because every hand has taken on nature's power,
And is beautifying the foul with false painted faces,
Authentic beauty no longer has a name or sacred place to be,
But is abused, if it doesn't already live in disgrace.
My mistress' eyebrows are black as ravens,
And her eyes are so dark, they seem like mourners,
As they sadly look on those who, while not born fair, do not lack beauty,
And who give beauty a bad reputation by using false means:
Yet her black eyes are so attractive in their sadness,
That now everyone says beauty should look that way.

Sonnet CXXVIII

How oft, when thou, my music, music play'st,
Upon that blessed wood whose motion sounds
With thy sweet fingers, when thou gently
sway'st
The wiry concord that mine ear confounds,
Do I envy those jacks that nimble leap
To kiss the tender inward of thy hand,
Whilst my poor lips, which should that harvest
reap,
At the wood's boldness by thee blushing stand!
To be so tickled, they would change their state
And situation with those dancing chips,
O'er whom thy fingers walk with gentle gait,
Making dead wood more blest than living lips.
Since saucy jacks so happy are in this,
Give them thy fingers, me thy lips to kiss.

How often when you, who are my music, play
music
Upon the blessed wood whose notes sound
Under your sweet fingers—when you gently
sway
The wiry tunefulness that amazes my ear—
I envy those keys of the harpsichord that leap up
nimbly
To kiss the tender inside of your hand,
While my poor lips, which should reap that
harvest,
Stand blushing at the wood's boldness toward
you!
To be so tickled, my lips would change their
position
And situation with those dancing keys,
Over whom your fingers walk with such a gentle
gait,
Making the dead wood more blessed than living
lips.
Since saucy keys are so happy in doing this,
Give them your fingers, and give me your lips to
kiss.

Sonnet CXXIX

The expense of spirit in a waste of shame
Is lust in action; and till action, lust
Is perjured, murderous, bloody, full of blame,
Savage, extreme, rude, cruel, not to trust,
Enjoy'd no sooner but despised straight,
Past reason hunted, and no sooner had
Past reason hated, as a swallow'd bait
On purpose laid to make the taker mad;
Mad in pursuit and in possession so;
Had, having, and in quest to have, extreme;
A bliss in proof, and proved, a very woe;
Before, a joy proposed; behind, a dream.
All this the world well knows; yet none knows
well
To shun the heaven that leads men to this hell.

*Spending the spirit in a waste of shame by
having sex
Is lust in action; and until it acts, lust
Gives false testimony, is murderous, rude, cruel,
and not to be trusted,
And is no sooner enjoyed than it is immediately
despised;
Hunted past reason, sex is no sooner had
Than past reason it is hated, like a swallowed
bait
Laid on purpose to make its taker crazy,
They are crazy in pursuit and in possession, as
well;
Had, having, and in quest of sex—they are crazy
the entire time;
Sex is ecstasy in the proving and—once
proved—a sadness;
Beforehand, it is an imagined joy; but
afterward, it is only a dream.
All of this, the world knows very well, yet no one
knows well enough
To shun the heaven that leads men to this hell.*

Sonnet CXXX

My mistress' eyes are nothing like the sun;
Coral is far more red than her lips' red;
If snow be white, why then her breasts are dun;
If hairs be wires, black wires grow on her head.
I have seen roses damask'd, red and white,
But no such roses see I in her cheeks;
And in some perfumes is there more delight
Than in the breath that from my mistress reeks.
I love to hear her speak, yet well I know
That music hath a far more pleasing sound;
I grant I never saw a goddess go;
My mistress, when she walks, treads on the ground:
And yet, by heaven, I think my love as rare
As any she belied with false compare.

My mistress's eyes are not like the sun at all;
Coral is much more red than the red of her lips;
If snow is white, well, then her breasts are grey-brown;
If hair is like fine wire, then black wires grow on her head.
I've seen roses that are pink, red and white,
But I don't see those colors in her cheeks;
And there is more delight in artificial perfumes
Than in the reek of the breath of my mistress.
I love to hear her speak, even though I know well
That music sounds much better than her voice;
I admit I never saw a goddess move;
My mistress, when she walks, tramples the ground:
And still, I swear to heaven, I think my love is as rare
As any that has been lied about through false comparisons.

Sonnet CXXXI

Thou art as tyrannous, so as thou art,
As those whose beauties proudly make them cruel;
For well thou know'st to my dear doting heart
Thou art the fairest and most precious jewel.
Yet, in good faith, some say that thee behold
Thy face hath not the power to make love groan:
To say they err I dare not be so bold,
Although I swear it to myself alone.
And, to be sure that is not false I swear,
A thousand groans, but thinking on thy face,
One on another's neck, do witness bear
Thy black is fairest in my judgment's place.
In nothing art thou black save in thy deeds,
And thence this slander, as I think, proceeds.

*You are as much like a tyrant as you are
Like those proud women whose beauty makes them cruel;
Because you know very well that in my foolish heart,
You are the fairest and most precious jewel.
Still, in all honesty, some people who look at you say
Your face does not have the power to make a lover groan.
I am not so bold as to say that they are wrong,
Although I swear it to myself to be true.
And, to prove it is not false, I swear
I made a thousand groans just thinking about your face,
A face on another's neck bears witness
That your dark complexion is the most beautiful as far as I'm concerned.
There is nothing dark about you except your actions,
And I think that is why people spread slander.*

138

Sonnet CXXXII

Thine eyes I love, and they, as pitying me,
Knowing thy heart torments me with disdain,
Have put on black and loving mourners be,
Looking with pretty ruth upon my pain.
And truly not the morning sun of heaven
Better becomes the grey cheeks of the east,
Nor that full star that ushers in the even
Doth half that glory to the sober west,
As those two mourning eyes become thy face:
O, let it then as well beseem thy heart
To mourn for me, since mourning doth thee
grace,
And suit thy pity like in every part.
Then will I swear beauty herself is black
And all they foul that thy complexion lack.

I love your eyes as they seem to pity me,
Knowing that the distain in your heart torments
me.
They have put on black like loyal mourners,
And look with pretty sympathy upon my pain.
And, honestly, the morning sun of heaven does
not
Flatter the grey cheeks of the east as well,
Nor does the full star that brings in the evening,
Do half the glory to the sober west,
As those two mourning eyes do to enhance your
face:
Oh, so then it is fitting to your heart
To mourn for me, since mourning favors your
looks,
And it would suit you as well to pity me with
every other part of you.
Then I will swear that beauty herself is black,
And everyone who does not have your
complexion is ugly.

Sonnet CXXXIII

Beshrew that heart that makes my heart to groan
For that deep wound it gives my friend and me!
Is't not enough to torture me alone,
But slave to slavery my sweet'st friend must be?
Me from myself thy cruel eye hath taken,
And my next self thou harder hast engross'd:
Of him, myself, and thee, I am forsaken;
A torment thrice threefold thus to be cross'd.
Prison my heart in thy steel bosom's ward,
But then my friend's heart let my poor heart bail;
Whoe'er keeps me, let my heart be his guard;
Thou canst not then use rigor in my gaol:
And yet thou wilt; for I, being pent in thee,
Perforce am thine, and all that is in me.

Curse you for causing my heart to groan
And for the deep wound you give to both my friend and me!
Isn't it enough to torture me alone,
Why should my friend also be brought into slavery to you?
Your cruel eye has taken me away from myself,
And my friend, who is like my second self, has fallen even harder:
By him, myself, and you, I've been abandoned;
Making a torment threefold unfold three times by being so deceived.
Imprison my heart in the steel cell of your bosom,
And let my poor heart serve as bail for my friend;
Whoever keeps an eye on me, let my heart be his guard;
That way you won't be able to be harsh in my jail:
And still, you will be, because I, being shut up inside you,
Of necessity am yours, and all that is in me is also yours.

Sonnet CXXXIV

So, now I have confess'd that he is thine,
And I myself am mortgaged to thy will,
Myself I'll forfeit, so that other mine
Thou wilt restore, to be my comfort still:
But thou wilt not, nor he will not be free,
For thou art covetous and he is kind;
He learn'd but surety-like to write for me
Under that bond that him as fast doth bind.
The statute of thy beauty thou wilt take,
Thou usurer, that put'st forth all to use,
And sue a friend came debtor for my sake;
So him I lose through my unkind abuse.
Him have I lost; thou hast both him and me:
He pays the whole, and yet am I not free.

So, now that I have confessed that he is yours,
And that I, myself, am mortgaged to your will,
I will give up myself if you give up my friend,
And return him to me so that he will still be my comfort:
But you will not, and he doesn't want to be set free,
Because you are possessive and he is kind;
He was wise and was backing me up with his name
And now that bond binds him just as firmly.
You will use the bond of your beauty to secure us,
You lender, that puts forth all to use,
And sues a friend who became a debtor for my sake;
So I have lost him through my unkind abuse.
I have lost him, and you have both him and me:
He pays for all of it, and still I am not free.

Sonnet CXXXV

Whoever hath her wish, thou hast thy 'Will,'
And 'Will' to boot, and 'Will' in overplus;
More than enough am I that vex thee still,
To thy sweet will making addition thus.
Wilt thou, whose will is large and spacious,
Not once vouchsafe to hide my will in thine?
Shall will in others seem right gracious,
And in my will no fair acceptance shine?
The sea all water, yet receives rain still
And in abundance addeth to his store;
So thou, being rich in 'Will,' add to thy 'Will'
One will of mine, to make thy large 'Will' more.
Let no unkind, no fair beseechers kill;
Think all but one, and me in that one 'Will.'

While other women have their desire, you have
your 'Will,'
And 'Will,' to boot, and 'Will' in excess;
I am more than enough to trouble you still,
And I will be adding another sweet thing to it
all.
Will you, whose lust is large and spacious,
Not even allow me to hide my will in you just
once?
Will the will of others seem true and good,
And on my will you will not even shine
acceptance?
The sea is full of water, and yet it still receives
rain,
And adds the abundance to its store;
And so you, being rich in 'Will,' can add to your
'Will'
My own will, to make your large 'Will' even
larger.
Don't kill a courteous suitor by being unkind;
Think of all of us as one, and accept me as one
'Will.'

Sonnet CXXXVI

If thy soul cheque thee that I come so near,
Swear to thy blind soul that I was thy 'Will,'
And will, thy soul knows, is admitted there;
Thus far for love my love-suit, sweet, fulfil.
'Will' will fulfil the treasure of thy love,
Ay, fill it full with wills, and my will one.
In things of great receipt with ease we prove
Among a number one is reckon'd none:
Then in the number let me pass untold,
Though in thy stores' account I one must be;
For nothing hold me, so it please thee hold
That nothing me, a something sweet to thee:
Make but my name thy love, and love that still,
And then thou lovest me, for my name is 'Will.'

If your soul stops you because I come so near,
Promise your blind soul that I am your 'Will,'
And will, or lust, as your soul knows, is admitted
there.
So far, for love, my wooing is sweetly fulfilled,
'Will' will satisfy the treasure of your love,
Yes, and it will fill it with will, and my will is
only one.
In things that can hold a lot easily,
Then one of anything is the same as none:
So, in the numbers you know, let me pass
uncounted,
Even though in the record of your holding, I
must be one;
Hold me for nothing, and may it please you to
hold
The nothing that is me, a something sweet to
you:
Make my name your love, and love it still,
And then you will love me, because my name is
'Will.'

Sonnet CXXXVII

Thou blind fool, Love, what dost thou to mine eyes,
That they behold, and see not what they see?
They know what beauty is, see where it lies,
Yet what the best is take the worst to be.
If eyes corrupt by over-partial looks
Be anchor'd in the bay where all men ride,
Why of eyes' falsehood hast thou forged hooks,
Whereto the judgment of my heart is tied?
Why should my heart think that a several plot
Which my heart knows the wide world's common place?
Or mine eyes seeing this, say this is not,
To put fair truth upon so foul a face?
In things right true my heart and eyes have erred,
And to this false plague are they now transferr'd.

Love, you blind fool, what are you doing to my eyes,
That they look at something and don't see what it is they see?
They know what beauty is and can see where it lies,
And yet they see the best when they are looking at the worst.
If my eyes distort things by seeing them with too much bias,
And are fixed in the common bay where all men ride,
Why have you used my eye's inaccurate vision as a hook
To catch the favorable opinion of my heart?
Why should my heart think that it has a separate place with her
When it knows that she belongs to the wide world as common?
Why do my eyes, when seeing this, say it is not so
And put a fair appearance upon such an ugly face?
My heart and eyes have made mistakes regarding the truth here
And now they are both caught up in this false illness.

Sonnet CXXXVIII

When my love swears that she is made of truth
I do believe her, though I know she lies,
That she might think me some untutor'd youth,
Unlearned in the world's false subtleties.
Thus vainly thinking that she thinks me young,
Although she knows my days are past the best,
Simply I credit her false speaking tongue:
On both sides thus is simple truth suppress'd.
But wherefore says she not she is unjust?
And wherefore say not I that I am old?
O, love's best habit is in seeming trust,
And age in love loves not to have years told:
Therefore I lie with her and she with me,
And in our faults by lies we flatter'd be.

When my love swears that she is made of truth,
I believe her, even though I know she lies,
And that she might think me some uneducated youth,
Unlearned in the false ways of the world.
Although she knows I am past my best days,
I simply give credit to her lying tongue:
On both sides, then, the simple truth is not told.
But what if she were to say that she is not a liar?
And what if I were that that I am not old?
Oh, love's best habit is in seeming to trust each other,
And loves prefers not to have its age told:
Therefore I lie with her and she with me,
And we flatter each other with lies despite our faults.

Sonnet CXXXIX

O, call not me to justify the wrong
That thy unkindness lays upon my heart;
Wound me not with thine eye but with thy tongue;
Use power with power and slay me not by art.
Tell me thou lovest elsewhere, but in my sight,
Dear heart, forbear to glance thine eye aside:
What need'st thou wound with cunning when thy might
Is more than my o'er-press'd defense can bide?
Let me excuse thee: ah! my love well knows
Her pretty looks have been mine enemies,
And therefore from my face she turns my foes,
That they elsewhere might dart their injuries:
Yet do not so; but since I am near slain,
Kill me outright with looks and rid my pain.

Oh, don't ask me to justify the wrong,
That your unkindness lays upon my heart;
Don't injure me with your eye, but do it with your tongue;
Use your power with power and do not slay me by using subtlety.
Tell me you love someone somewhere else, but when you are in my sight,
Dear heart, please hold off from glancing at others:
Why would you need to wound me with cunning when your power
Over me is more than I can possibly defend myself against?
Let me excuse you: oh, my love knows very well
Her pretty looks have been my enemies,
And, therefore, she turns my enemies away from my face,
So that they might aim their injuries somewhere else:
Yet, don't do this, since I am very near slain,
Kill me outright with your looks and rid me of my pain.

Sonnet CXL

Be wise as thou art cruel; do not press
My tongue-tied patience with too much disdain;
Lest sorrow lend me words and words express
The manner of my pity-wanting pain.
If I might teach thee wit, better it were,
Though not to love, yet, love, to tell me so;
As testy sick men, when their deaths be near,
No news but health from their physicians know;
For if I should despair, I should grow mad,
And in my madness might speak ill of thee:
Now this ill-wresting world is grown so bad,
Mad slanderers by mad ears believed be,
That I may not be so, nor thou belied,
Bear thine eyes straight, though thy proud heart go wide.

Be as wise as you are cruel; do not test
My speechless patience with too much distain;
Otherwise, my sorrow might give me words and
the words will express
The nature of my pain, which wants pity.
If you allow me to give you some advice, it
would be better
If you do not tell me, love, if you do not love me;
In the same way that sick men who are short-
tempered and whose deaths are near,
Are not told about the state of their health even
though their doctors know;
Because if I should feel despair, I will go crazy,
And in my craziness, I might speak badly of you,
And now that this world that twists the truth has
grown so bad,
Crazy slanderers are believed by crazy people
who hear them,
So that I may not be like that and lie about
you—
Keep your eyes directly on me, even though your
proud heart may widely stray.

Sonnet CXLI

In faith, I do not love thee with mine eyes,
For they in thee a thousand errors note;
But 'tis my heart that loves what they despise,
Who in despite of view is pleased to dote;
Nor are mine ears with thy tongue's tune
delighted,
Nor tender feeling, to base touches prone,
Nor taste, nor smell, desire to be invited
To any sensual feast with thee alone:
But my five wits nor my five senses can
Dissuade one foolish heart from serving thee,
Who leaves unsway'd the likeness of a man,
Thy proud hearts slave and vassal wretch to be:
Only my plague thus far I count my gain,
That she that makes me sin awards me pain.

To be sure, I do not love you with my eyes,
Because they see a thousand errors in you;
It is my heart that loves what they despise,
Who, in despite of the view, is pleased to be a
fool;
My ears are not very delighted by the sound of
your voice,
And I don't necessarily have tender feelings
when touching you,
Neither my sense of taste nor smell desire to be
invited
To any sensual feast with you alone:
But neither my mind nor my five senses can
Persuade my foolish heart from serving you,
My heart leaves my body to stand here alone
looking like a man,
While it goes off to be the wretched slave to your
heart:
I only gain one thing from this illness
And that is that the one who makes me sin
awards me with pain.

Sonnet CXLII

Love is my sin and thy dear virtue hate,
Hate of my sin, grounded on sinful loving:
O, but with mine compare thou thine own state,
And thou shalt find it merits not reproving;
Or, if it do, not from those lips of thine,
That have profaned their scarlet ornaments
And seal'd false bonds of love as oft as mine,
Robb'd others' beds' revenues of their rents.
Be it lawful I love thee, as thou lovest those
Whom thine eyes woo as mine importune thee:
Root pity in thy heart, that when it grows
Thy pity may deserve to pitied be.
If thou dost seek to have what thou dost hide,
By self-example mayst thou be denied!

Love of you is my sin and your best virtue is hate,
You hate my sin that is grounded in sinful loving:
Oh, but compare your state to my own state,
And you will find my state is not in need of rebuke;
Or, if it is, not from those lips of yours,
That have abused their red ornamentation of lipstick,
By sealing false bonds of love with a kiss as often as mine,
And have robbed others' beds and lovers of what is due to them.
It is right that I love you as you love those
Whom your eyes woo in the same way that mine beg you:
Plant pity in your heart for me, so that it grows
So that if you need pity, you may deserve to be pitied, as well.
If you seek to have what you yourself do not show,
By your example, you may not receive it, either!

Sonnet CXLIII

Lo! as a careful housewife runs to catch
One of her feather'd creatures broke away,
Sets down her babe and makes an swift dispatch
In pursuit of the thing she would have stay,
Whilst her neglected child holds her in chase,
Cries to catch her whose busy care is bent
To follow that which flies before her face,
Not prizing her poor infant's discontent;
So runn'st thou after that which flies from thee,
Whilst I thy babe chase thee afar behind;
But if thou catch thy hope, turn back to me,
And play the mother's part, kiss me, be kind:
So will I pray that thou mayst have thy 'Will,'
If thou turn back, and my loud crying still.

Listen! In the same way that a careful housewife runs to catch
One of her hens that has broken away,
And sets down her baby to make a quick run
In pursuit of the thing she does not want to get away,
While her neglected child chases after her,
And cries to catch the attention of the busy mother who is focused
To follow after the thing that flies before her face,
With no awareness of her poor baby's unhappiness;
In the same way, you run after that which flies away from you,
While I, like the baby, chase far behind after you;
But if you catch the one you're hoping for, then turn back to me,
And play the mother's role—kiss me and be kind:
And I will pray that you may have your 'Will,'
If you turn back and silence my noisy crying.

Sonnet CXLIV

Two loves I have of comfort and despair,
Which like two spirits do suggest me still:
The better angel is a man right fair,
The worser spirit a woman colour'd ill.
To win me soon to hell, my female evil
Tempteth my better angel from my side,
And would corrupt my saint to be a devil,
Wooing his purity with her foul pride.
And whether that my angel be turn'd fiend
Suspect I may, but not directly tell;
But being both from me, both to each friend,
I guess one angel in another's hell:
Yet this shall I ne'er know, but live in doubt,
Till my bad angel fire my good one out.

*I love someone who comforts me, and someone
who makes me despair,
They are like two angels who make constant
suggestions to me:
The better angel is a man who is right and fair,
And the worse angel is a woman who is colored
ill.
To win me over toward hell, the evil female
Tempted my better angel from my side,
And will corrupt my saint until he is a devil,
Wooing his purity with her foul confidence.
And whether my angel has turned into a fiend—
I suspect it to be true, but I can't directly tell;
But since they are both away from me and being
friendly with each other,
I guess one angel is in another's hell:
Still, I will never really know, but live in doubt,
Until my bad angel burns my good one out of
hell.*

Sonnet CXLV

Those lips that Love's own hand did make
Breathed forth the sound that said 'I hate'
To me that languish'd for her sake;
But when she saw my woeful state,
Straight in her heart did mercy come,
Chiding that tongue that ever sweet
Was used in giving gentle doom,
And taught it thus anew to greet:
'I hate' she alter'd with an end,
That follow'd it as gentle day
Doth follow night, who like a fiend
From heaven to hell is flown away;
'I hate' from hate away she threw,
And saved my life, saying 'not you.'

Those lips that Love's own hand created
Breathed out the sound that said 'I hate'
To me that wasted away for her sake;
But when she saw my sorry state,
Mercy came into her heart right away,
Scolding that tongue that is always sweet
But was used in delivering a gentle judgment,
And she taught it how to say something new:
She altered the phrase 'I hate' with an ending,
That followed the words like a gentle day
Follows night, who like a devil
Is thrown away from heaven into hell;
'I hate' she threw away from hate,
And saved my life by adding 'not you.'

Sonnet CXLVI

Poor soul, the centre of my sinful earth,
[ ] these rebel powers that thee array;
Why dost thou pine within and suffer dearth,
Painting thy outward walls so costly gay?
Why so large cost, having so short a lease,
Dost thou upon thy fading mansion spend?
Shall worms, inheritors of this excess,
Eat up thy charge? is this thy body's end?
Then soul, live thou upon thy servant's loss,
And let that pine to aggravate thy store;
Buy terms divine in selling hours of dross;
Within be fed, without be rich no more:
So shalt thou feed on Death, that feeds on men,
And Death once dead, there's no more dying
then.

Poor soul, that lives in the center of my sinful
body,
[ ] these rebel powers that dress you up.
Why do you feel longing inside and suffer
shortage,
While painting your outward appearance with
such expensive things?
Why do you put out such a large amount of
money when you have such a short lease,
And spend it upon your fading mansion?
Will worms, the inheritors of this excess,
Eat up your outlay? Is this how your body will
end?
Then, soul, you should live upon your servant's
loss,
And let the body long while you build up your
supplies;
Buy time in heaven by selling hours of rubbish,
And feed your inside, not allowing the outside to
be so rich:
In this way, you will feed on Death, which feeds
on men,
And once Death is dead, there will be no more
dying then.

Sonnet CXLVII

My love is as a fever, longing still
For that which longer nurseth the disease,
Feeding on that which doth preserve the ill,
The uncertain sickly appetite to please.
My reason, the physician to my love,
Angry that his prescriptions are not kept,
Hath left me, and I desperate now approve
Desire is death, which physic did except.
Past cure I am, now reason is past care,
And frantic-mad with evermore unrest;
My thoughts and my discourse as madmen's are,
At random from the truth vainly express'd;
For I have sworn thee fair and thought thee bright,
Who art as black as hell, as dark as night.

My love is like a fever, longing still
For that thing that makes the disease last longer,
And feeding upon what will make the illness stay,
With an uncertain and sickly appetite to satisfy.
My reason, which is the doctor to my love,
Is angry that his prescriptions are not being kept,
And has left me, and, desperate now, I confirm
That desire is death, which medical science expected.
I am past cure and my reason is past care,
And I am frantic-mad with constant unrest;
My thoughts and conversation are like a madman's,
Uselessly expressing random truths;
I would have sworn you were beautiful and I thought you were bright,
But you are as black as hell, and as dark as night.

Sonnet CXLVIII

O me, what eyes hath Love put in my head,
Which have no correspondence with true sight!
Or, if they have, where is my judgment fled,
That censures falsely what they see aright?
If that be fair whereon my false eyes dote,
What means the world to say it is not so?
If it be not, then love doth well denote
Love's eye is not so true as all men's 'No.'
How can it? O, how can Love's eye be true,
That is so vex'd with watching and with tears?
No marvel then, though I mistake my view;
The sun itself sees not till heaven clears.
O cunning Love! with tears thou keep'st me blind,
Lest eyes well-seeing thy foul faults should find.

Oh my, what eyes has Love put into my head,
Which have no correspondence with true sight!
Or, if they have, where has my judgment gone,
That wrongly judges what they see right?
If what my eyes dote on looks beautiful to me,
What does it mean when the world says that's not the case?
If it's not, then love would do well to distinguish
That Love's eye is not as accurate as all men's 'No.'
How can it be? Oh, how can Love's eye be true,
When it is so troubled with watching and with tears?
It's no wonder, then, that I mistake my view;
The sun itself does not see until the skies clear.
Oh, cunning Love! With tears you keep me blind,
Because well-seeing eyes would find your ugly faults.

Sonnet CXLIX

Canst thou, O cruel! say I love thee not,
When I against myself with thee partake?
Do I not think on thee, when I forgot
Am of myself, all tyrant, for thy sake?
Who hateth thee that I do call my friend?
On whom frown'st thou that I do fawn upon?
Nay, if thou lour'st on me, do I not spend
Revenge upon myself with present moan?
What merit do I in myself respect,
That is so proud thy service to despise,
When all my best doth worship thy defect,
Commanded by the motion of thine eyes?
But, love, hate on, for now I know thy mind;
Those that can see thou lovest, and I am blind.

Can you, oh cruel woman, say that I don't love you
When I take sides with you against myself?
Don't I think about you, even when I forget
To think about myself for your sake, you tyrant?
Who hates you that I would call my friend?
Is there anyone I delight in that you frown upon?
No, if you scowl at me, don't I expend
Revenge upon myself with moaning?
What quality do I respect in myself,
That would make me so proud to despise being your servant,
When all of the best of me worships your worst,
And you can command me with a simple motion of your eyes?
But, love, go ahead and hate me, because now I know your mind;
You love those who can see, and I am blind.

Sonnet CL

O, from what power hast thou this powerful might
With insufficiency my heart to sway?
To make me give the lie to my true sight,
And swear that brightness doth not grace the day?
Whence hast thou this becoming of things ill,
That in the very refuse of thy deeds
There is such strength and warrantize of skill
That, in my mind, thy worst all best exceeds?
Who taught thee how to make me love thee more
The more I hear and see just cause of hate?
O, though I love what others do abhor,
With others thou shouldst not abhor my state:
If thy unworthiness raised love in me,
More worthy I to be beloved of thee.

What power gives you the powerful ability you have
To be able to control my heart even though you are so inadequate?
To make me lie about what I really see,
And swear that the day is not bright when it is?
Where did you get this ability to make bad things look good,
So that even in the very worst of your actions,
You guarantee so much strength and skill
That, in my mind, your worst is better than all the best?
Who taught you how to make me love you more
The more I hear and see good reason to hate you?
Oh, even though I love what others despise,
You shouldn't despise my love for you the way others do:
Since your unworthiness makes me love you,
Then I'm the one who is most deserving of your love.

Sonnet CLI

Love is too young to know what conscience is;
Yet who knows not conscience is born of love?
Then, gentle cheater, urge not my amiss,
Lest guilty of my faults thy sweet self prove:
For, thou betraying me, I do betray
My nobler part to my gross body's treason;
My soul doth tell my body that he may
Triumph in love; flesh stays no father reason;
But, rising at thy name, doth point out thee
As his triumphant prize. Proud of this pride,
He is contented thy poor drudge to be,
To stand in thy affairs, fall by thy side.
No want of conscience hold it that I call
Her 'love' for whose dear love I rise and fall.

Love is too young to know right from wrong,
But doesn't everyone know that love gives you a conscience?
So, gentle cheater, don't go on too much about what I've done wrong,
In case your sweet self turns out to be guilty of the same faults:
Because you have betrayed me, I, in turn, betray
My higher self to my lowly body's needs.
My soul tells my body that it may
Find joy in sex; my flesh doesn't wait to hear any more reasons;
At the sound of your name, flesh rises and points you out
As his glorious prize. Swollen with pride
He is happy to be your poor worker,
And to stand up to tend to your business and then fall down by your side.
It is not necessarily due to lack of conscience that I call
The woman whose love makes me rise and fall
'Love.'

Sonnet CLII

In loving thee thou know'st I am forsworn,
But thou art twice forsworn, to me love
swearing,
In act thy bed-vow broke and new faith torn,
In vowing new hate after new love bearing.
But why of two oaths' breach do I accuse thee,
When I break twenty? I am perjured most;
For all my vows are oaths but to misuse thee
And all my honest faith in thee is lost,
For I have sworn deep oaths of thy deep
kindness,
Oaths of thy love, thy truth, thy constancy,
And, to enlighten thee, gave eyes to blindness,
Or made them swear against the thing they see;
For I have sworn thee fair; more perjured I,
To swear against the truth so foul a lie!

By loving you I know I am breaking a promise I made,
But you, in swearing to love me, are breaking two promises:
You are breaking your wedding vows by cheating and your promise
Of love to your new lover by swearing to hate him.
But how can I accuse you of breaking two promises,
When I break twenty? I perjure the most,
Because all of my promises are only told to deceive you.
All of my real trust in you is gone,
Because I have sworn deeply that you are so kind,
And have sworn of your love, your faithfulness, and you constancy,
And, to make you look better, I blinded myself to your faults
And made my eyes swear they did not see what they saw;
Because I have sworn you are beautiful, I am more of a liar,
And have sworn against what is true after telling such an awful lie!

Sonnet CLIII

Cupid laid by his brand, and fell asleep:
A maid of Dian's this advantage found,
And his love-kindling fire did quickly steep
In a cold valley-fountain of that ground;
Which borrow'd from this holy fire of Love
A dateless lively heat, still to endure,
And grew a seething bath, which yet men prove
Against strange maladies a sovereign cure.
But at my mistress' eye Love's brand new-fired,
The boy for trial needs would touch my breast;
I, sick withal, the help of bath desired,
And thither hied, a sad distemper'd guest,
But found no cure: the bath for my help lies
Where Cupid got new fire--my mistress' eyes.

Cupid set down his flaming torch and fell asleep:
A maiden of Diana's took advantage of the situation
And soaked his love-igniting fire
In a cold mountain stream that was nearby.
The stream borrowed from the holy fire of Love
A live-giving heat that is eternal, and so still endures,
And the stream became a bubbling bath, which men still find
Offers an outstanding cure against strange diseases.
But at a glance from my mistress, Love's flaming torch fired up again,
And, to test it out, Love touched it against my breast;
I was made sick by this, and desired the help of the stream's bath,
And I hurried into it as a sad and sick guest,
But I found no cure there: the cure for my distress lies
Only in the place where Love got his new fire: my mistress's eyes.

Sonnet CLIV

The little Love-god lying once asleep
Laid by his side his heart-inflaming brand,
Whilst many nymphs that vow'd chaste life to keep
Came tripping by; but in her maiden hand
The fairest votary took up that fire
Which many legions of true hearts had warm'd;
And so the general of hot desire
Was sleeping by a virgin hand disarm'd.
This brand she quenched in a cool well by,
Which from Love's fire took heat perpetual,
Growing a bath and healthful remedy
For men diseased; but I, my mistress' thrall,
Came there for cure, and this by that I prove,
Love's fire heats water, water cools not love.

The little Love-God Cupid once fell asleep
After placing his heart-inflaming torch by his side.
Several nymphs that had vowed to remain chaste for life
Came skipping by, and one of them,
Who was the most beautiful, picked up the fire
Which had warmed the hearts of armies of true lovers;
And so the leader of hot desire
Was asleep when a virgin disarmed him.
She extinguished the torch in a cool pool water nearby,
Which absorbed the perpetual heat of Cupid's fire
And became a bath that provides a healthy remedy
For men who are diseased; but I, enslaved to my mistress,
Came there for the cure and tested the waters to find:
Love's fire heats water, but water does not cool love.

Made in United States
Orlando, FL
12 March 2023